Steve —
more about Quantitative through Quantative than can ever be expressed!

The Long Walk Here
A Short Prehistory of Humanity

G.E.Will

Gregory E. Williams

Published through CreateSpace
an Amazon company, Delaware, USA

To contact the author email: longwalkhere@gmail.com

Copyright © 2018 Gregory E. Williams. All rights reserved.

ISBN-13: 978-1722605179
ISBN-10:1722605170

DEDICATION

Dedicated to my mother, Bertha Pauline Vessell, who constantly encouraged me to explore new things, to question almost everything, to get out of the house and play in the dirt, and to appreciate even the smallest of things that life has to offer in our short time here.

CONTENTS

	Acknowledgments	
	Introduction	1
Ch 1	The Study of Prehistory	5
Ch 2	Archaeology as Anthropology	8
Ch 3	Science as a Way of Knowing Things	14
Ch 4	Origins, Bipedalism and Dispersal	28
Ch 5	Hunting and Gathering	48
Ch 6	After The Ice Melted	58
Ch 7	States and Civilizations --Rise and Fall	64
Ch 8	Southwest Asia and Mesopotamia	70
Ch 9	The Mediterranean	80
Ch 10	Europe	86
Ch 11	Egypt and Africa	94
Ch 12	South and Southeast Asia	104
Ch 13	China and East Asia	112
Ch 14	Australia and the Pacific	120
Ch 15	North America	128
Ch 16	Mesoamerica and the Caribbean	136
Ch 17	South America – Andes and Amazon	148
Ch 18	Conclusion	158
Ch 19	Postscript	160
Ch 20	The Lakh Clock	166
	References	176
	List of Tables	189
	List of Figures and Illustrations	189
	About the Author	190

ACKNOWLEDGMENTS

I acknowledge with pleasure my debts to many students, colleagues and friends for their inspiration, patience, and encouragement over the several years that it took to write this book.

I presented much of this material to my classes of undergraduates at the University of Colorado Denver where I occasionally teach an introductory course on archaeology (how we do it) and an upper level class on world prehistory (what we found out). The students' questions and comments helped me figure out what was important to non-archaeologists and what was not. This helped me figure out what not to put in the book. The faculty in the anthropology department (particularly Tammy Stone and Christopher S. Beekman) provided me with supportive, challenging, and thoughtful comments as this project unfolded. Special thanks to Charles Musiba for letting me use his personal photograph of the Laetoli footprints on the cover. Any shortcomings, errors, or omissions are strictly of my own doing.

I want to thank Dana Stillman of Inspire Graphics for her creative work on the interior graphics and the cover design and I recommend her to others searching for similar cost-effective and inspirational talent.

I also am deeply indebted to many friends and colleagues whose conversations over the decades have helped me figure out, to at least a small extent, why archaeology matters to us as we live our lives and do what we do before we finally join our ancestors. Thanks particularly Richard Murphy who provided many insights as an Alaska Native and who is an expert hunter-gatherer who can find a ripe berry anywhere within a half mile, and to Peter Minahan for reading an early version of this book.

In alphabetical order by last name I extend my gratitude to Kathy Beekman, Harrison Coerver, Kay Colmorgan, John Cuellar, Kevin Gerrits, Bob and Judy Farley, Bob and Sue Guttman, Jonathan Kent, Marty and Richard Martin, Scott Meiklejohn, Peter and Beth Minahan, Andy Morehead, Brian O'Neil, Carol Patterson, Bruce Rippeteau, Peter Stevinson, George and Lynn Rockwell, Rick Rought, Joan Tezak, Connie Turner, Greg Walcher, and Jay Wilson.

INTRODUCTION

Life can only be understood backwards; but it must be lived forwards. Soren Kierkegaard

This book is about humans, it is about us ... and it is based on the archaeological evidence that we have at hand.

It has three main purposes and is intended for those who are not specialists in archaeology. One is to present what we think we know about the past in a short narrative, one is to demonstrate the vast time scale involved in prehistory, and one is to discuss why we care about the past

Archaeology is not only about our past, it is also about our future. I believe that we can better understand the present based on what we know about the past. With this important knowledge, we at least we can stop kidding ourselves about what we know about things that are largely dust now. Our past does not determine not our future, but it is our past, we are curious about it, and hopefully we can learn a few things from it.

The one major lesson from history is that "men do not learn very much from the lessons of history" (a quote attributed to Aldous Huxley). I hope to contribute to the seemingly fruitless effort to change this by attempting to make archaeology more relevant, and in the words of Kenneth Feder (2007), put the "past in perspective".

Modern politicians, pundits, journalists, observers, and others love to cite the past to support their arguments, but they often do so out of context or with limited knowledge, and actually this gives me hope because it underscores why archaeology matters to so many people. Most of us seem to want to anchor our modern agenda on something we think happened in the distant past, ethnic, genetic, religious, social, political, economic, technological, militaristic, or otherwise; and so clearly the past matters today.

This book attempts to address the questions of who we are, where we come from and to a degree, why are we here, and where we are going, from an archaeological perspective. Archaeology is an evidence-based social science. So, this is about what we know today based on what we have discovered in the last century and a half (or so) of scientific endeavor.

I have done everything I can think of to make it as readable as possible without getting too deep into archaeological jargon or theory. I chose the metaphor of going for a long walk because walking on two feet is one of the earliest defining features of being human and because I am a huge fan of Bill Bryson and his book *A Walk in the Woods* (1998). Also see his great book *A Short History of Nearly Everything* (2003). Like Bryson I will tell a story and we will meet a few concepts and ideas along the way that will hopefully make this book interesting.

We are an incredible species that excels at manipulating and adapting to our natural and imagined environment and we have had many ups and downs over the last several millennia. Some people think we are the best thing that ever happened to our planet Earth, others say the opposite. I withhold judgment on that but you will see in this book I think our story is just really beginning to unfold.

Archaeology is the study of prehistory through the material record left behind. Archaeology employs many tools of science and yet is more than a science; it is also part of the humanities and is concerned with real people actually living in the past. So, this book is about is how we can shape the present in a big way or maybe just use the information to shape our individual lives and perhaps spark some curiosity.

For example, humans have been walking upright for our entire existence. It is only in the last few decades that most of us have spent more time sitting than standing or walking. There is evidence this is not so great for our health but this comes as no surprise to me because there are very few chairs in the archaeological record.

One thing about the study of the past that amazes my students is how very, long ago some things happened and how a lot of time went by when things basically changed little. For this reason, I developed a very simple timeline that does not have to be adjusted in a visual scale to be useful. I call the Lakh clock. Every second in a 24 hour "day" equals one calendar year. One minute therefore equals 60 years, and one 24-hour day on the Lakh clock equals 86,400 actual years. This is close enough to 100,000, which is the definition of "Lakh" in Sanskrit for me. It sure beats calling it the "86,000-plus year clock".

This way (on the cumulative timeline in Chapter 20) I have put important events in context by converting them to a time point on the imaginary Lakh clock. It is likely not original, others have used similar ways to approach this, yet I have not found this particular year-to second-conversion ratio in the literature. It seems to work well, I have tried several other methods (generations, fractions, and so forth) but this resonates with my students.

This book will begin with some basics about archaeology then we will examine the human fossil record and the dispersal of humanity across the globe (our ancestry). We also address key technological innovations (like stone tools, pottery, and then agriculture) and the rise of complexity and the associated social transformations (like states) on each continent. The book ends with a discussion of some thought elements that relate to us today.

One of the "take-aways" of this book will be that in our study of the past one thing we typically do is to underestimate the ingenuity and imagination of our ancestors. As the story unfolds hopefully you will be thirsty for more detailed information available from a wide range of credible academic and popular sources. See the references at the end for plenty of good reading.

My major sources for this work are my lecture notes based on textbooks and my readings of scholarly books and articles. I routinely vary the textbooks I use in my classes and this means we benefit from the work of great scholars such as Fagan (2010), Fedder (2007), Haviland (2002), Omohundro (2008), Scarre (2013), Wenke and Olzewski (2007), and even

Kotler (which is a marketing textbook with wonderful insights into consumer behavior). In a sense this book is a synthesis of early syntheses.

As such, I owe a special debt to both Scarre (and his chapter contributors, because he was the editor) and Fagan and Durrani. In the words of Matt Walters (who wrote an excellent book on the Persian Empire), "Rather than cite them on almost every page, I will acknowledge my deep debt to their work here, as frequent sources of information and inspiration in this writing." (Walters 2014:xiix). As such there are few, if any, original concepts in this book, which is largely a synthesis, and which has not undergone strict peer-review (it is more like a blog … in print). However, I do take an author's liberty of humbly suggesting a few areas where the current view might be due for re-examination.

Also, this book is not comprehensive and can never be completely up to date. But archaeology is an ever-changing field focused on an ever changing (transitory and adaptive) creature (us).

When you have read this book, you will have the basics to evaluate most popular archaeology articles or programs you might read in the newspaper or see on television or the internet (even the ones about "space aliens"). I started writing this book several years ago and incorporated as many recent discoveries as I could but some are just too recent to mention. As I tell my students, "read, read, read" and you might keep up on things.

While you read through the regions and timelines I strongly suggest that you also take the time to visit this website, *www.timemaps.com* (or something similar) where you can get a visual image of the culture groups, states, and empires, by region, around the globe over the last several thousand years. I also encourage you to conduct an internet search for key topics and images (for copyright reasons I do not include many images). Try to focus on web sites with a .edu, .gov, or .org url.

For expeditious reasons I have used the English translation of most place names. I apologize in advance for this and hope to correct it is a future edition, if any.

1 THE STUDY OF PREHISTORY

Technically prehistory is the study of the time before writing based on the material record.

But archaeologists also use written texts to assist their efforts when they can. So basically, we have prehistoric archaeology and historic (text aided) archaeology. Sometimes the written and material records coincide. Sometimes they do not. Often, this is where it gets really interesting because the stories they produce may actually be in serious conflict, and this leads to a greater understanding of what happened long ago.

Some of the earliest investigations into prehistory involved armchair philosophizing and lots of speculation. In about 1650 a scholar named James Ussher, Archbishop of Armagh in Ireland, tried something new (Bahn 1998, 2003). Using the bible as his source (he had few other sources) he established the creation of the world at noon on October 23, 4004 BCE (see below for an explanation of "BCE" and other dating conventions). Many people scoff at his work because they are under the mistaken assumption he merely added up all the lineages in the Old Testament. First, let us put his work into context. In 1650 when he made this claim the only sources of information available to scholars were the bible and some Greek texts, he had no material archaeological data to use. For his time he was a revolutionary thinker.

Ussher relied on the generally accepted notion that one day in the realm of God was a thousand years. So, Ussher assumed that the six days of God's creation lasted 4,000 years before the birth of Christ (and would endure 2,000 years after it). The extra four years came from an adjustment based on Herod's death in 4 BCE, which made that the year of Christ's birth (on his scale). Other complications involved considerations relating to the beginning of the year (he chose the Jewish year which begins in autumn). After a lot of work Ussher chose the first Sunday after the autumn equinox, which was October in the Julian calendar as his start date. This has since been converted into the Gregorian calendar, which is no small feat. Noon, it seems, was an arbitrary selection on his part but it provides symmetry.

Ussher deserves a lot of credit for his work. We now know that he greatly underestimated the age of the world but at the time his proposed origin date seemed incredibly old. The story of prehistory in this book begins about 3.6 million years with some of the oldest evidence of upright walking. It generally ends about 500 years ago, depending on the region, and in some areas like the Pacific the story continues into the late eighteenth century.

The archaeological story of our past is not fiction. It is based on the material record, on evidence. As such it is like an investigative news story. It is concerned with the Who, What, When, Where, How and sometimes with Why certain things happened certain ways. The story of our past can be considered an informed narrative and it is constantly unfolding as new evidence arises.

The history of archaeology involves several phases. Into the 17th century those interested in the distant past had little more than speculation to go on, at least until Ussher's seminal work. The late 17th and 18th centuries were largely a period where wealthy antiquarians (land owners with leisure time) collected curiosities from the past but they had no way to determine how old these items were. The late 18th and early 19th century saw a period of global exploration by Western powers and the development of the first efforts to systematically investigate ancient ruins. By the early 20th century archaeology was firmly established as an academic specialty and our efforts largely focused on identifying and classifying materials from the past. Elaborate taxonomies classifying pottery, stone tools, and other items were constructed. These were often more fanciful then real because they were largely based on the world views of the Western archaeologists who studied them, not the world views of the people who made them.

With the introduction of Carbon 14 dating (in 1949) for the first-time archaeologists could date organic materials from anywhere in the world. This was a milestone because until then we had some idea that certain types of things were older than certain other types, but we had no way of knowing how much older they actually were. Carbon 14 (radiocarbon) dating changed that forever. In the intervening time, we have refined this dating method and added several other ways of dating ancient materials to our toolbox. Incidentally this is why archaeologists talk about years before the present. By the present we mean 1950 because that is the reference date for all Carbon 14 dating. So sometimes you will see things that are "years ago", others are "Before Present" (1950), and others are "BC" (not used here) or "BCE" which means Before Common Era (largely defined as the birth of Christ). I chose to use the "BCE" notation in this book but it can also be read as "BC" (Renfrew and Bahn 2008, 2010).

The second half of the 20th century saw an explosion of archaeological research and the widespread application of the methods of science to the study of the past. In North America archaeology was housed in the anthropology department, in Europe it was generally in the history department or as a part of the study of the classics (such as Greece and Rome).

Archaeology underwent an existential crisis in the 1980's where two "camps" took aim at each other. One was the "processual" school that focused its studies on adaptation, subsistence, and resource utilization of large prehistoric populations through an overarching cultural and environmental "process" approach. The other was the "post-processual" school that took a stronger interest in and a focus on individual agents in the past and the "lived environment" of antiquity (Binford: 1962, Flannery:1967, Hodder 1982, Hodder 1991a, Hodder1991b, Yoffee 1993). Since then there has been a sort of truce between the two and a bit of a melding.

2 ARCHAEOLOGY AS ANTHROPOLOGY

What is anthropology? Technically it is the study of humankind. It is concerned with what people do and why they do it. In North America most departments of anthropology have adopted the "four field" approach that includes cultural anthropology, biological anthropology, linguistics, and archaeology.

Cultural anthropology studies living human societies in their physical environment. Cultural anthropologists typically live with the group they are studying, sometimes for a year or for several years off and on. They learn the language and they observe their behavior. This is called "participant observation". Cultural anthropologists produce reports on their observations called "ethnographies".

Biological anthropologists are concerned with two basic aspects of people. One relates to the physical and medical characteristics of living, breathing humans. The other one relates to the fossil record and the study of human origins through fossil bones and tools produced by our distant ancestors, and sometimes genetics (when ancient deoxyribonucleic acid commonly called "DNA" is available). Biological anthropologists are concerned with everything from HIV/AIDS, to obesity, to the lives of our human ancestors. The study of our ancestry through the fossil record is often called paleoanthropology.

Linguists study human communication through language. Right now there are Approximately 7,000 languages spoken on the face of the planet but at the current rate of change estimates suggest that we are losing two or three languages every few weeks as indigenous populations adopt Western ways and the older generations die off. At this rate in a century there will be just a few hundred languages left. This is very important because language and our perception of the world have been demonstrated to be tightly interwoven and so we are rapidly losing different ways of looking at the world, communicating about it, and appreciating it.

Archaeologists study past human activity based largely on the material record. This is a book about the temporal perspective of our past from an archaeological perspective. I will have more to say about what archaeology is and what we have found out in the rest of this book.

The Concept of Culture

The concept of "culture" is critical to anthropology. What is culture? This is an important question. Like many important concepts, it is somewhat ambiguous. Anthropologists view humans as cultural creatures. Yes, there is a large biological aspect to our behavior so we can say humans are "bio-cultural" but no biological human exists without a cultural background (unless they have been raised in isolation or have developmental issues beyond the scope of this book).

But still, what is culture? In 1952 an anthropologist named Clyde Kluckhohn co-authored a book where he and his colleague Alfred Kroeber identified over 150 uses of the term culture.

It constantly amazes me that many undergraduate anthropology majors have no working definition of culture in their minds. I ask this question all the time so I know that most do not. In the popular vernacular culture means being "cultured" and attending operas, receptions, hanging out with rich people, or going to wine and cheese parties (tongue-in-cheek here). To be cultured in the Western world differs greatly from having "culture" in an anthropological sense.

There is also the concept of "popular" culture (working people) as opposed to the "high" culture of the elites. There is also the concept of subcultures such as a "youth culture" or a "survivalist culture", or an "urban" culture for example. The list goes on and on. We have a culture of inclusiveness at this bank, we have a culture of respect here, and we have a culture of discipline in the military … and so forth.

People who try to manipulate "culture" for corporate or organizational purposes generally think of culture as something imposed from above. For example, here is an imaginary scenario: "Executive memo #204, Everyone will be cooperative, work harder, and be punctual". In a way they are right, culture comes from outside us, but it comes from the actions and beliefs of other people in our society we regularly interact with, and from us. What many "pointy haired managers" (from the cartoon series "Dilbert") forget is that people are not un-aware of this and a "sub-culture" within the larger corporate culture (a culture of resistance) will likely develop when things are imposed from above.

We will publicly behave "as if" what is said is the right thing (See *Denial* by Varkii and Brower). But we may also develop something called a "culture of resistance" which is very important in the archaeological record, but very hard to identify. It is sometimes associated with the collapse of complex institutions, such as those big states that I will discuss later.

So, what is culture? A working definition I use is "culture is our learned and shared norms, values, ideals, and beliefs that are transmitted primarily through language" (Omohundro 2008). A shorter version is "culture is our shared way of believing and behaving." It is one of the most powerful characteristics of humanity.

A classic definition was crafted in 1870 by Edward Tyler, "Culture ... is that complex whole which includes knowledge, belief, art, morals, law, custom, and any other capabilities and habits acquired by man as a member of society" (See Omohundro and Haviland for more on this). Other definitions suggest that culture is that which distinguishes one group of people from another ... which raises very interesting questions about who we consider ourselves to be and who or what we consider other people to be.

Learned and shared is key; and transmitted through language is key. Humans are not born with any one cultural perspective; we learn and MUST share our cultural perspective. We are born with the innate ability to do this, so for us culture is a biological imperative. For the learning to be useful it must be shared during our lives. And language (sound) is the principal way we transmit this. We also share a lot of information through nonverbal symbolism, and through imitation and that is why it is important for us to socialize.

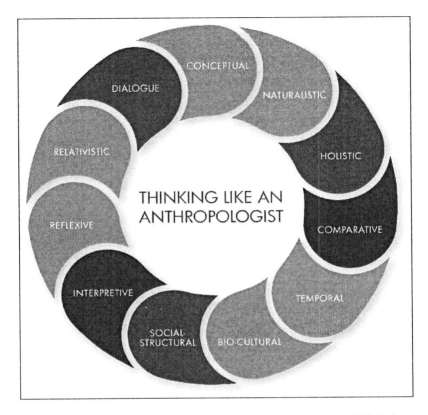

Figure 1. This represents the ways that anthropologists investigate and think about our world. It is not meant to be read left to right or right to left. It merely illustrates the approaches that anthropologists incorporate into their work (Omohundro 2008).

Thinking Like an Anthropologist

Anthropological thinking involves several approaches. Remember that no one anthropologist employs each approach equally in their work and some are more focused on certain approaches than others. The key to thinking holistically (in an anthropological sense) is to know of and to respect each of the different approaches and to recognize that they are not mutually exclusive. There is high overlap between them. For this outline, I am indebted to John T. Omohundro, whose textbook *Thinking Like an Anthropologist* was my mainstay when teaching Introduction to Cultural Anthropology.

The circular illustration highlights these various approaches to doing and understanding anthropological fieldwork.

Conceptual.   The conceptual approach means understanding the anthropological concept of culture and having a good working definition at hand.

Naturalistic. The naturalistic approach involves observing human behavior in our natural environment, just as a trained biologist would observe animals in their natural habitat. Many cultural anthropologists are trained in participant-observation where they live among the people they are studying for a prolonged period.

Comparative.   The comparative approach means having first-hand experience with more than one culture, speaking more than one language, and a sophisticated knowledge of geography. The comparative approach is often concerned with cross-cultural and multi-cultural studies.

Temporal.   The temporal approach means understanding the vast time depth of human prehistory. This is largely the realm of archaeology and paleoanthropology. This book is largely temporal in its approach.

Bio-cultural.   The bio-cultural approach largely views humans as biological creatures living in a cultural realm where culture is our principal adaptive strategy. Biological and socio-cultural aspects of human behavior are more or less equally important in this approach.

Social-structural.   The social-structural approach is largely focused on questions associated with status, roles, hierarchies and human social structures ranging from the relatively simple to the highly complex. The social-structural approach is interested in social transformations, power, gender, age, economics, and politics. Sometimes this is called a socio-political or socio-economic approach.

Interpretive.   The interpretive approach is largely concerned with symbolism. This approach recognizes that symbols will often have more than one meaning and that the meanings are communicated through verbal and non-verbal methods. There is an existential (how do we know what we know) element to the interpretive approach that recognizes that what is believed to be true in one context or society may not be viewed the same way in another society.

Relativistic.   The relativistic approach is largely concerned with the relationship between values and morality. Cultures are viewed in their own context and under this approach and it is generally agreed that one culture cannot be judged by the values of another culture. This approach does not mean that one society is more evolved or "better" than another and it does not imply that all societies must inevitably transform themselves into complex states. This concept is sometimes called cultural relativism.

Dialogue. The dialogue approach engages in communication with others without being judgmental. Native voices, descendant populations, gender, identity, and multi-vocality are all accepted as important sources of information and ideas.

Reflexive. The reflexive approach is largely an introspective approach. It requires the observer to question his/her own viewpoint. The reflexive approach is concerned with the interplay between culture and individuals rather than to accept culture as something big and unchanging that is externally imposed.

Holistic. The holistic approach is acutely aware of context and the interplay between the different approaches mentioned above. The holistic approach is concerned with the way different aspects of life interact such as culture, environment, technology, and beliefs.

Remember, no one way to look at "us" is the "right" way. This primer is only meant to familiarize you with the many ways that anthropologists work. In this book we are mostly focused on the temporal, comparative, bio-cultural, and socio-structural (or socio-political) approaches.

3 SCIENCE AS A WAY OF KNOWING THINGS

What is science? Many people are confused about this. Largely, science is about gathering reliable information and testing hypotheses. It is also about taking your results and make predictions or at least make informed generalizations. It is not about "proving" things.

It is not about measuring everything that you observe and hoping for an answer to jump out at you (as most graduate students wish). It is a way of knowing things based on evidence that can be perceived by at least one of the senses (empiricism) and every new discovery typically generates several new questions (Kuhn1970, Ziman 1988).

There is a wonderful book series and movie called *Hitchhikers Guide to the Galaxy* which makes this point very well. The answer to a paraphrased question to a mega-computer "what is the ultimate answer everything" (after measuring everything) … is not "42" (which is what their computer said). When queried, the computer basically said "ask a silly question get a silly answer" (Barber 2005).

It is also important that your scientific work can be replicated by other scientists. Different scientific disciplines employ their own terminology and practices for their work but the overall "umbrella" is the basically same.

One thing that scientific endeavors cannot do is to ignore contrary evidence. This is a big no-no. Political visionaries, religious leaders, attorneys, and conspiracy theorists excel at this and it serves them well (Bestman and Gusterson 2005), but in science you cannot just connect the dots you want to, you must account for, or at least acknowledge evidence that you cannot account for, and you must look for and sometimes find dots that may be hard to see or hidden behind other dots, and that makes it even more complex and interesting.

In this section I will introduce a few basic points about scientific methodology and the theory behind it. There is a lot of public misconception about science and scientists themselves will often disagree about certain things.

For example my friends in the world of the physical and chemical sciences like to refer to what they do as "hard" science. They often note that the social and behavioral sciences, like anthropology, are "soft" sciences because we cannot usually predict outcomes. I like to remind them that their units of measurement (atomic or sub-atomic particles or chemical compounds) will usually do the same things in similar conditions every time because they lack something called volition. They cannot decide things for themselves. They are largely "reactive".

In the social and behavioral sciences, our subjects are humans and other animals and they are quite capable of doing things that one would not expect. Sometimes they lie, sometimes they change their minds, and sometimes they just stop talking to us and go do something else. So, which science is "hard"? I argue that social and behavioral sciences are "harder" than the physical and chemical sciences because our subjects do unpredictable things (Bernard 2002). My glib response is more than just a play on words.

This argument will likely not get resolved soon, but it underlies an important point or two. First, gathering information through observation is key to all scientific work. For a century, naturalists like Darwin "just" collected samples and organized them. Cultural anthropologists go into the field and "just" gather information, largely through something called "participant observation".

The fact that two anthropologists working in the same society arrive at different conclusions does not negate the important basic research they are conducting. One could be a male and the other a female, and by that sexual distinction they will be allowed access to different aspects of any one culture's activity. They could be visiting the same people years apart and witnessing the changes that occurred in one society over time, and that will influence their observations. One researcher could be interested in subsistence strategies and the other in kinship relationships so they will be focusing on different aspects of the same culture. This does not negate their work; it makes it stronger because our debates and discussions about the different results of social and cultural research allow us to understand the process and the people better.

Physics has a similar problem because the very act of observing sub-atomic particles (using light) alters the trajectory of those particles. Basically the "flashlight" that we use to observe them projects such strong energy that it moves them. So, are we observing their "pristine" behavior or their modified behavior? Is there a way to observe any pristine sub-atomic behavior? Actually, there is some very creative research on this very question going on right now.

This is an interesting question because when a cultural anthropologist lives with a group of people, to observe them, the people know about the anthropologist and may often alter their behavior in order to obtain their own (often unstated) desired results.

So, do we stop doing basic research? No. We cannot. That is why it is called "basic". What we can do is develop a more sophisticated understanding of what purposes it can or cannot be used for and how far we can (or should) stretch it. In this regard, I say such basic observational and descriptive research as essential to science. Some scientists disagree with me. They say that fieldwork without a testable hypothesis is not science. I say there is no way to develop the question you want to test without knowing something about the environment you are studying. I will leave the details of this argument for another day (for more on this see Babbie 2004, Johnson 1998, Louden 2006; Bernard 2002, and Feigl 1988).

So in this book I will include things like ethnographies in the general umbrella of science. Trust me, many ethnographers and cultural anthropologists who deal regularly with the vagaries of the human experience would prefer to not be included in a chapter on science and scientific method. I understand and respect their positions but to understand prehistory I must include them and their important work in this book.

Another point I will make is that science is actually a sub-discipline of philosophy. There is something called "The Philosophy of Science" (Boyd 1999, Ziman 1988) and it deals with what science can and cannot accomplish. It is based on the relatively modern concepts of empiricism and rationalism. It is concerned with what we observe and how we make sense of those observations. Plato (Rowe 2005), Descartes (Damasio 1994, Gluck 2007), and Kant (Rader 1976) had a lot to say about this.

Discussions about this quickly move into another realm, which is the realm of what is real and what is perceived to be real. What is real? Is it real because we can see and measure it? What about the things we can't see and can only measure when they have left a trace behind? Were they real or is just what is left real? This gets us into questions that are existential (having to do with the basics of knowledge as humans, my opening quote in this book was from an existentialist) and epistemological (how we know what we know).

Briefly, let me say that in the words of Frank Zappa, "Everyone believes in something" (Zappa n.d). And this is an important statement because I want to distinguish between what is real and what is not for the purposes of this discussion. Some say that reality is what is left when you stop believing. Need I believe in gravity for it to be real? No. It does not matter if something is physical or social when talking about human cognition (and perception) because to us they are all equally real in influencing our behavior.

I could use this concept to demonstrate that money is not real. It does not grow on trees, like apples. Ours is a fiat economy, and our financial system is based on the concepts of safety and soundness, trust, and confidence. When these fail, as they nearly have recently (2007 and 1929), then the entire system fails. In a sense our modern economy works because most of us believe in it or at least we accept that we cannot change it individually so we act "as if" (Varki and Brower 2013) it was real. In archaeology, it is important to try to understand this and to try to understand what the people in the past believed in, if possible.

I have intentionally left out discussions of metaphysics and religion because they are, by definition, beyond the realm of science. They are not beyond the realm of scientific investigation into human behavior and are strongly within the realm of archaeology. Religion is extremely important in understanding human prehistory. You cannot, I would argue, understand a human without discussing religion or our appreciation of something we call the "supernatural" because it is part of the human experience (Durkheim 1995(1912), James 2004(1902), and Rappaport 1999).

Science is also about ordering and organizing things in the natural world so they make sense to us. It is a way of knowing things. For example, in biology something called the Linnaean Taxonomic System is commonly used. For our purposes in this book we begin with genus, then progress to species and subspecies. The genus is generally capitalized, and the species and subspecies are not, and they often end in an "s". All are customarily italicized. For example, *Homo sapiens neanderthalensis* refers to the Neanderthals as a subspecies of *Homo sapiens*. *Homo neanderthalensis* refers to the Neanderthals as a distinct species. This represents two distinct ways of categorizing the same creature. I will say more about this later because I think when we do it we might be focusing too much on physical characteristics and not enough on culture.

In science data is very important. When conducting research it is very important to know what kind of data you will be collecting because different statistical and analytical tools can only be used with certain types of data (Kachigan 1986, Thomas 1976). No one type is "better" than another type, they are just simply different. Some are more "robust" than others because they are less affected by perturbations in the data set. Some even argue that qualitative methods are more "robust" than many quantitative methods because the qualitative narrative upon which the quantitative work is based doesn't change (Patton 2002; Wylie 1985).

The most basic data type is called "nominal data". Basically, it organizes categories by name. A good example is "present or absent" or "male or female". This is also a binary data set, and often more complex data is "reduced" to "binary" form through a process called dichotomization. It is important to know that more complex data can be dichotomized but dichotomized data cannot be made more complex. It is data in its most basic form and one category is not "better" or "worse" or "higher" or "lower" than another category, they are just different.

The next category in complexity is called "ordinal data". We have all seen ordinal data in surveys where we are asked to rank something on a scale of 1-5 where one is terrible, two bad, three is acceptable, four is exceptional, and five is excellent (or something like that). Trust me there are many variations on these labels and the fact that they are each one increment apart does not mean that the respondent views the scale as an even one. We have also seen these scales on a 1-10 level and even on a 1-3 level. A grading scale ranging from "F" to "A" is a Likert scale (of a relatively unique kind because the values are also percentages and the scales for each category are not all equal).

For example, and most students realize at least part of this, an "F" is anything between 0 and 59 points. A "D", "C", or "B" is defined by a 10-point spread but an "A" has an 11-point spread (90-100). Go figure.

The next category in complexity is called "interval data". We all use interval data every day. An example is measuring temperature. Both the Fahrenheit and Centigrade scale have arbitrary zero points but the intervals are equal. Some might say Centigrade has a fixed zero point (when water freezes) but actually that depends on atmospheric pressure. The only absolute temperature scale would begin at absolute zero (such as Kelvin), but again we have other physical and environmental issues to consider. As a "teaser" here let me say there is a way to turn a Likert scale into a make-believe interval scale, but it only works if you set your Likert scale up properly at the outset and if you admit that you do not know if the distances between the intervals are real or imagined.

The final category is a ratio scale. Think of a ruler. There are equal intervals and there is a fixed zero point. Measuring height or width is always done on a ratio scale, regardless of whether it is in inches, centimeters, or any other equal unit (like Egyptian cubits).

So, in the science of measuring things we have four choices. Actually we have five. The first one is descriptive or qualitative. Then we can break down the items identified through description into one of four categories for measurement discussed above. Think of description as the foundation of the science pyramid and data as the next tier up on that foundation.

Variables are what is being measured, like height and weight in the example above. Values are the actual measurements associated with each variable. So if we have a sample of 20 people and we measure two variables for each person (height and weight) we come up with 40 values in our dataset. The larger your sample size the larger your dataset will be.

In an experiment know your variables, and what type the measured values of the variables will be. It is also important to know the difference between an independent variable and a dependent variable (the dependent variable is the one that scientists watch when they modify the independent variable in an experiment).

It is also often useful to establish a control group you can use to compare to the changes to your experimental group. Sometimes these experiments are set up so carefully nobody, including the researcher, knows which is which to avoid any unintentional interference by the research team. This is called a "blind" or a "double blind" experiment and is common in the pharmaceutical industry but is less common in archaeology (Nance 1987).

Two basic statistical concepts are important to develop a solid foundation in observation and science. One is percentages. We all use percentages when we calculate tips at a restaurant. It is very useful to include percentages in our narratives of the past. This is a descriptive statistic. Many people are not comfortable calculating percentages in their head. In my introduction to archaeology class I usually have my students calculate the percentage of certain types of artifacts in an overall collection of materials from an excavation. To my surprise about 33% of undergraduates cannot accurately calculate percentages without a little practice.

The other is ratios. What is the ratio of one type of tool to another type of tool in a site? A hammer is a tool, so are nails. Do we expect a ratio of 1:1 between hammers and nails? No, that would be silly. But what is the ratio? Is it 1:1000? This might seem like a basic question but when trying to figure out how people lived in the distant past we often want to ask questions about the relationships between different things they made and used and what they are made out of and possibly how they were made. We use frequency distributions (basically charts listing the quantities of things) to arrive at percentages and ratios, in a way frequency distributions are one of the most powerful tools of science.

I hope this helps you see that science is a tool. It is not absolute. It is a way of knowing things, at least for a while (until new discoveries are made). It is one of many ways of understanding our world. I like to think that science is the best method we have come up with so far to keep us from fooling ourselves.

Let me give you a very simple example. Presume there are three ways that people can view the world. Each is illustrated by one circle below. I have conveniently labeled it the *Tripliciter Sciendi Scenario* but I probably should have called it the *Duas Vias, et Scienta Scenario* (two views and the science view).

Circle A (in Figure 2 below) represents what we learned culturally as a child. This is called enculturation. We don't even remember learning it. This is sometimes called "origin amnesia" and it occurs because our brains were still largely developing while we were engaged in learning the very first things in life. The world seems to "fit" because we were taught to think of things as fitting together in certain ways and we don't remember thinking any other way, because we never thought any other way.

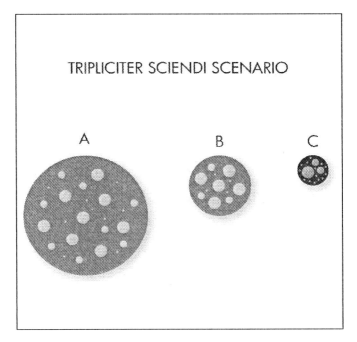

Figure 2. An illustration of various ways people "connect the dots" in their life ranging from enculturation (A), to life experiences (B), to science (C). © Gregory E. Williams, 2018.

Anybody who visited another culture as an adult probably experienced something called culture shock. This is because different cultures have different ways of dealing with and explaining similar physical and social things in the environment, and when we experience new cultures we learn new ways of connecting things, sometimes it can be a shocking experience.

A simple example is driving on the "wrong" side of the road. People from the United States visiting Great Britain sometimes die because they look at the incoming and outgoing traffic, in the wrong lanes, and confidently step right in front of an oncoming vehicle. This is just a simple example of how different cultures work and about how we are such cultural creatures.

Circle B represents our tendency to connect the dots ourselves based on our own personal observations of the world and our life experiences. It is how we try to make sense out of things. It is smaller than circle A because we do less of it, possibly.

We all engage in Circle A and Circle B thinking, usually without even thinking about it. It is the foundation for the way we live our daily lives. It forms the core of our values and beliefs. Some have said that if you challenge somebody's beliefs about the way the world works you better make them laugh, otherwise they will kill you, because we take this "natural" way of viewing the world very seriously. We can all think of examples of this in the modern geo-political world.

When we connect the dots in our physical or social environment in new ways we often ignore the dots that do not fit, and sometimes we cannot even see all the dots. It is a useful and expedient, but not thorough way of organizing the way we look at the world.

Political and religious visionaries engage in this process often, so do attorneys (in fact they are trained to ignore certain dots, especially when defending a client, this falls under something called the discovery process and rules of evidence). Conspiracy theorists and political pundits also excel in this type of thinking (Bestman and Gusterson 2005). It is not "bad". It can be highly useful, particularly when a leader must quickly identify potential threats. It is just not heavy on the nuances or the details.

In a way Circle A and Circle B are the glue that hold people together and that also separates them. They represent the ongoing dynamics of social discourse (some civil some not) and interaction.

For example, many modern professional and trade associations have a board meeting and get the basic business done in about half an hour but the meeting goes on and on for the allotted time. At the end someone sighs and says "we didn't **DO** anything in this whole meeting". They are largely wrong, the officers and participants spoke and interacted with each other, and that matters in terms of understanding each other getting along … it matters a lot.

Circle C represents scientific inquiry. It is the smallest circle because fewer of us do it (Goldenberg 1992). It is the one that keeps me awake at night. Presuming our methodology was excellent and we made no errors in our data collection and analysis, but if our sample was a bad one or our methods were not up to the task, we can actually fool ourselves into believing we are right when we may not be. The entire world saw an example of this when most of the "scientific" polls failed to accurately predict the outcome of the 2016 United States presidential election.

We have statistical procedures that help us figure out how likely we are to be correct. But they only work if our sample is good. This is why sampling, replicability, and peer review are so important in science. If my results cannot be replicated by another scientist, then something is most likely amiss. If my peers do not agree with my methods or interpretation then something may be amiss (or I may just be a genius, but that is unlikely). Maybe I am on to something new that could cause the re-interpretation of the evidence, perhaps a new theory about this or that or a "paradigm shift" (Kuhn 1970) that defines what theories are likely to hold water. But that is very unlikely.

With these examples I hope you see that scientific discovery is an ongoing and iterative process, and that it is a tool for us to learn (not a substitute for social interaction, including religion, as some would suggest). For more on this see Archer and Bhaskar et al. 1998.

Some have said that half the science out there is bad science; the problem is we do not know which half. I would suggest that the small part that has not been replicated or subjected to peer review is a likely candidate.

Here is a diagram that incorporates the fundamentals of what we have discussed earlier with discovery and data at the foundation.

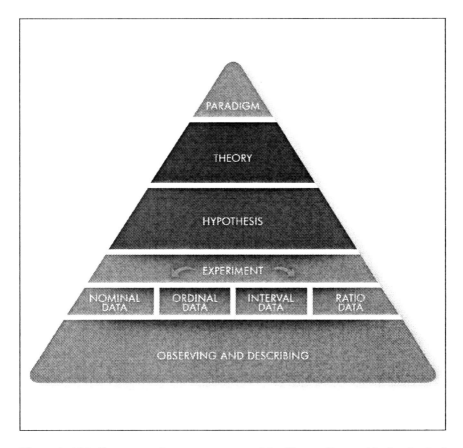

Figure 3. This illustrates an important concept. Scientific paradigms guide theories (and schools of thought), theories guide testable hypotheses, hypotheses guide experiments, experiments rely on data, and data comes from observation and description. But where do paradigms come from? © Gregory E. Williams 2018

Culture, as I defined it earlier, is a learned and shared set of norms, values, ideals, and beliefs transmitted primarily through language. Paradigms are our culturally influenced ways of theorizing how our world works. Paradigms help us define what we are interested in investigating and they insulate us from the temptation in science to simply measure everything.

A paradigm shift occurs when the accumulated evidence no longer supports the prevailing theories. Geology recently (in the 1950's) experienced this with the acceptance of plate tectonics to explain how continents move. When I was in grade school I asked my teacher when South America and Africa split apart (because they "matched" on her global map on the wall so well) and she said I was asking a silly question because everyone knows continents could not move and that I needed to stop asking such questions. She clearly wasn't "up" on the latest paradigm shift that had been around for a decade or more. I felt stupid and stopped asking questions in her class (but after the school year we moved to another state and all was well). Theories are our way of formulating broad concepts under general paradigms. For more on scientific revolutions, paradigms and theories, see Kuhn 1970.

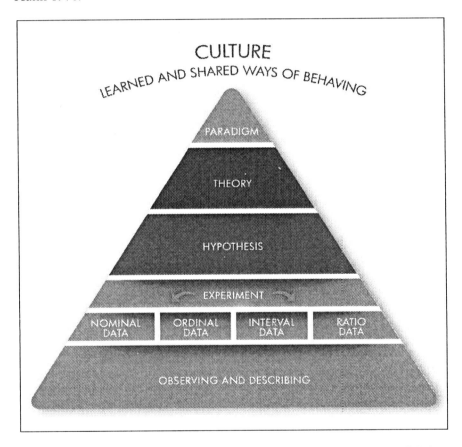

Figure 4. In this final diagram, I am trying to illustrate that culture is the "umbrella" that overarches science, even though science can transcend and even modify our various cultural views. Our norms, values, ideals, and beliefs guide our scientific endeavors and sometimes, they cloud our vision, in other cases they enhance it. Science does not happen in a vacuum devoid of human experience and the scientific questions we invest our time and resources on are largely determined by our culture in a complex interplay with our natural environment. Culture is indeed a powerful thing in the realm of human experience. © Gregory E. Williams 2018.

We are all cultural creatures living in a physical environment. I hope this makes sense to you because it is fundamental to understanding almost everything that follows in this book. Our subjects of investigation are dead and gone and usually they left no written records for us. Sometimes when they did and we still cannot decipher them, but they lived and died in a world full of shared cultural meaning.

Remember that our Western world view, which is largely the result of the age of Enlightenment (and all the science I mentioned above), was probably **not** shared by the ancient people we are investigating. They had different cultural traditions and they seem to have connected the dots in their world in a very different fashion than we do, and these were often in wild and wondrous ways.

While we may never fully understand the experience of actually living and surviving and maybe even thriving in prehistory, we must constantly remind ourselves that the way we interpret the material culture (that is our only evidence of the past) is largely subject to our own cultural experience, biases, predispositions, and stereotypes.

Archaeology questions everything, even the process of archaeology (Tilley 1990). It can be no other way if it is to be even somewhat objective. This is part of what makes it so exciting and it is why it is so relevant to today. The example I gave you above about money and how it is not "real" is a good case in point. We treat it "as if" it was real and we do not give it a second thought. Maybe there is a lesson here in the way we look at prehistory too. It has been said (I am paraphrasing here) that "reality has little to do with what is actually real". I find this to be intriguing.

Now you have a basic understanding of science and the scientific method that underlies so much of what archaeologists do. Archaeology is about finding out things that tell us about the past and in the process we discover new things about ourselves. It is not about the stuff, it is about the story.

So, let the story begin.

THE LONG WALK HERE

Table 1. Origins, Bipedalism, Dispersal and Cognition - Timeline
Unless otherwise stated dates are the beginning or earliest dates

Event	Approximate Date	Lakh Time where one second equals one year (times are Approximate)
Today		11:59 pm
Sputnik 1, Space Age Begins	AD 1957	11:58 pm
Holocene Begins	11000 BCE	7:37 pm
Homo floresiensis disappears	15000 BCE	7:17 pm
Glacial Maximum	11000 BCE	7:02 pm
Humans Reach North America (roughly)	16000 BCE	7:00 pm
Neanderthals disappear (roughly)	25,000 years ago	5:01 pm
Dogs Domesticated (perhaps)	32,000 years ago	3:07 pm
Chauvet Rock Art	32,000 years ago	3:07 pm
Humans Colonize Australia by Sea	45,000 years ago	11:30 am
Denisovans Appear	50,000 years ago	10:07 am
Modern Human Behavior (roughly)	75,000 years ago	3:10 am
Homo floresiensis appears	95,000 years ago	Yesterday
Neanderthals appear (roughly)	150,000 years ago	2 days ago
Antinomically Modern Humans Appear	200,000 years ago	2.3 days ago
Controlled Use of Fire (roughly)	250,000 years ago	3 days ago
Schoningen Spears	300,000 years ago	3.5 days ago
Homo naledi	335,000 years ago	4 days ago
Homo heidelbergensis	600,000 years ago	7 days ago
Language (inferred)	1.7 million years ago	20 days ago
Homo erectus Appears	1.7 million years ago	20 days ago
Homo ergaster Appears	1.7 million years ago	20 days ago
Genus *Homo* Appears (*H. habilis*)	2 million years ago	Three weeks ago
Australopithecines disappear	2 million years ago	Three weeks ago
Bipedalism	3,600,000 years ago	A month and a half ago
Pliocene Epoch	5,300,000 years ago	Two months ago
Humans and Chimps Split (est.)	8,000,000 years ago	Three months ago
Primate Dispersal	23,000,000 years ago	One year ago
Primates Appear	33,900,000 years ago	Just over a year ago

4 ORIGINS, BIPEDALISM, AND DISPERSAL

Humans are primates, and primates are mammals. Let us start here. The Order Primate includes the new and old-world monkeys and the apes. Primates originated in the Oligocene epoch which began approximately 33,900,000 years ago.

Several characteristics of primates include stereoscopic (binocular) vision, a reduction in the size of the canine (fang) teeth, the loss of claws and the appearance of fingernails, and the ability to grasp things like tree branches with the hands and sometimes with the feet. Primates are also generally social creatures who exist in small groups, sometimes called "bands".

Primates originated in Africa when the continent was connected to what is now the Americas. We see monkeys in both the new and old world but we find apes and early human ancestors only in Africa. Primate diversification and dispersal was a major characteristic of the Miocene epoch which began approximately 23 million years ago, after the continents had drifted apart.

In the Pliocene epoch we see the appearance of a new group of primates called hominins (basically ancestors to modern humans) and hominids (basically other primate groups). The hominin family (the way the classification system goes from largest to smallest is order, family, genus, species) includes the ancestors of modern humans. The Pliocene epoch began Approximately 5,300.000 years ago.

Sometime between about 5 million years ago and 8 million years ago the human line (hominins) and the chimpanzee line (hominids) split. The gorillas (hominids) split from the chimpanzee-human line about 8 million years ago. Although not ancestral to humans (we likely share a common ancestor), chimpanzees are our closest living relatives on this planet, we share more than 99 percent of our genetic material with them, although it is arranged differently in our chromosomes.

As large terrestrial primates living in a savanna (prairie) environment these creatures faced many adaptive challenges. One of the major adaptive features of this time was the appearance of the ability to walk on two feet (bipedalism).

Bipedalism provided several advantages to our ancestors. It allowed them to move between ecological niches and to take advantage of a much broader range of food, and to access distant food sources relatively quickly (Leakey 1994, Stringer 2012, Sussman 1999, Tattersall 2012). By "climbing down from the trees" we gave up our arboreal (tree) roots and expanded into new territories. By freeing up our hands we could carry things and, perhaps more important, we could throw things to ward off predators.

We also eventually grew in stature to what is close to the height of modern humans and were able to use our binocular vision (as primates) to see over the tall savannah grass into far horizons. Bipedalism is a way of moving that is configured for endurance rather than power or speed (like a Leopard). It is highly efficient for wide-ranging foraging. There is also a theory this is when our ancestors lost their full body covering of hair. This hair loss, combined with the ability to sweat, allowed them to regulate their body temperature more efficiently in a tropical or sub-tropical environment and therefore provided greater mobility.

The story of our journey in this book literally begins with our ability to walk upright, which dates to Approximately 3.6 million years ago. This marks the beginning of our "Long Walk Here".

Genus *Australopithecus*

Although there may be other undiscovered species of early hominins we are beginning with the Australopithecines. The Australopithecines were fairly short (by modern standards) upright walkers with relatively long arms and small brains and are found in East and South Africa. One site possibly associated with them is of particular interest because it consists of a length of parallel footprints of perhaps two or three upright walkers.

The Laetoli footprints (see the cover image on this book) were made in fresh volcanic ash sometime between 3.58 and 3.75 million years ago), possibly by *Australopithecus afarensis*. The date is confirmed through a technique called potassium-argon dating. There are other footprints of small animals and insects in the same location. There are also splash marks in the solidified volcanic ash that may have been made by raindrops. This site, in Tanzania, is a World Heritage site and was discovered by Mary Leaky in 1976.

One of the most famous Australopithecus fossils is "Lucy" which was found in the nearby Hadar region of neighboring Ethiopia. Lucy was approximately 3.5 to 4.0 feet tall. The skeleton is named Lucy because the famous Beatles song of the same name was reportedly playing on the radio when the excavators uncovered her.

Lucy is affectionately (but incorrectly) known as the "grandmother of humanity" based largely on her ability to walk upright (and other physical characteristics). A key skeletal characteristic of bipedalism is the angle where the head of the femur connects with the hip bone (innominate). This determines the carrying angle of the lower legs and is known as the "bicondylar angle". It usually measures approximately 135 degrees and we see a similar angle in modern human skeletons. Lucy had a bicondylar angle that suggests she was an upright walker.

There are various other species of australopithecines including *Australopithecus africanus* and *Australopithecus garhi*. These are all "gracile" australopithecines. Another, more robust group of australopithecines, has also been identified in the same region. These include *Australopithecus boisei* and *Australopithecus robustus*. By about 2 million years ago Australopithecines had disappeared from the fossil record as a species.

We are not certain that they are ancestral to humans but at this point there are no other likely candidates in the fossil record. There is no direct evidence that the australopithecines made tools, although some recent discoveries suggest that perhaps toolmaking was associated with *Australopithecus garhi*.

Australopithecus garhi stood about 4 feet 10 inches tall and had a brain about a third the size of a modern human (a bit larger than Lucy). The legs are long and humanlike, but the arms are long and more like those of Lucy (and some apes). The lower molars are about three times the size of a modern human and this suggests a diet consisting of coarse fibrous plant foods.

Genus *Homo* – *Homo habilis*

Our genus, *Homo* (meaning "similar" or "man"), first appears in the fossil record in East Africa a little more than 2 million years ago (roughly the time the australopithecines disappeared).

Homo habilis is the oldest "archaic human" on a short list. The species was discovered, and named, by Louis and Mary Leakey in 1960, and has a larger brain and smaller teeth than the australopithecines. It stood about 4 feet 3 inches tall and weighed perhaps 88 pounds. This means that *H. habilis* was slightly smaller than some australopithecines.

Four criteria are generally used to assign a bipedal fossil to the genus *Homo*. One is a brain size of about 600 cubic centimeters, the possible possession of language, the possession of a precision grip with an opposable thumb, and associated stone tools. Recent discoveries may change the way we think about this (Semaw 2000).

How do we know the volume of a fossil brain? There are several methods to determine this but just think about filling all the holes in a complete skull and then pouring in a jar full of sand or peas. Empty the contents into a beaker or measuring cup and you will have a general idea of the volume of the brain. Modern humans have a brain volume of approximately 1,200 cubic centimeters (cc) so in ordered to be considered a part of the genus *Homo* a fossil must have a brain at least about half the size of a modern human.

Another way to think of this is that the Australopithecines had a brain about the size of a large orange, while modern humans have a brain about the size of a small cantaloupe.

How do we infer language from the fossil record? That is more difficult but the potential for language is implied by absolute brain size and by the presence of stone tools.

Homo habilis seems to have had the ability to "map" resources over the local landscape and has clearly been associated with toolmaking. The tools associated with *Homo habilis* are "Oldowan" tools and this technique basically involves striking a stone made of a suitable material with another stone and chipping off a few sharp flakes that can be very, sharp cutting instruments (for more on stone toolmaking see Andrefsky 2005, Odell 2004, Whittaker 1994).

The technique is not as complex as later stone toolmaking methods but it is replicable and effective, it is also not associated with any other genus of hominins (although some recent research suggests that chimpanzees may occasionally make stone tools). The ability to find stones of a suitable material somewhere in the local environment, then carry them (or flakes made from them) to a different location suggests a detailed knowledge of the landscape.

The early sites in the Olduvai region suggest that stone and food resources were carried to a "central place". In this remote time our distant ancestors appear to have developed a practice that became characteristic of later hunter-gatherers who would periodically move from one base camp to another after marginally depleting the local resources within about a 5 kilometer or three-mile radius. This represents about an hour's walk on a flat landscape.

Genus *Homo* – *Homo ergaster*

By the beginning of the Pleistocene epoch (about 1.7 million years ago) we see the appearance of a new species of human in tropical Africa. This was a very arid period; much of the water on the surface of the earth was locked up in massive ice sheets in the polar regions.

Homo ergaster's overall skeletal proportions (including height) were much more like those of modern humans. Something that *Homo ergaster* may also have tamed fire (although the oldest clear evidence of intentional fire dates to only about 250,000 years ago) and appears to have migrated over long distances in Africa, but not into Asia (for more on fire and us see Wrangham 2009). One particular skeleton, discovered by Richard Leakey and Alan Walker, is a virtually complete specimen that lived about 1.6 million years ago on the shores of Lake Turkana.

Known as the "Turkana boy" this individual is estimated to have been about eleven years old when he died. His brain was about 130 cc larger than *Homo habilis* and his body proportions were strikingly similar to that of modern humans. If he had lived to adulthood he likely would have grown to about six feet in height.

Genus *Homo* – *Homo erectus*

Considered a descendent of *Homo ergaster*, the earliest *Homo erectus* fossils also date to approximately 1.7 million years ago. They were first found in

Java in Southeast Asia and used to be known as "Java man" or *Pithecanthropus erectus* (when I was an undergraduate).

Homo erectus has a brain larger than *Homo habilis* and may be the first human species to have migrated out of Africa. If so, the early migration route was likely north across the Sahara Desert (which was habitable at the time) then east into Asia but not north into the then frigid regions of Europe or eastern Asia.

Homo erectus is associated with the Acheulian stone toolmaking tradition, which followed the Oldowan tradition mentioned earlier. Acheulean hand axes are bifacially flaked (flaked on both sides) and come in many materials but they all tend to follow the same general tear drop proportions. The tradition lasted nearly a million years and if there was ever a strong candidate for a "logo" for our technological and engineering abilities as humans it would be the Acheulean handaxe. This is the only image other than the cover that I am including in this book, it is so important.

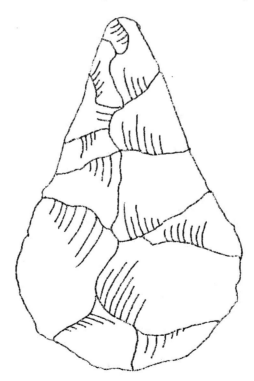

Illustration 1. Acheulean Handaxe. Drawing by Gregory Williams based on a sketch by John Frere, 1800.

It is interesting that the Acheulean handaxes are found associated with *Homo erectus* remains in western Asia but not in eastern Asia. One school of thought about this discrepancy is that bamboo and wood were preferred for tools in the east, but they do not preserve well in the archaeological record. The line demarking the boundary between stone tool and bamboo tool technology is the "Movius Line" and it cuts roughly through the middle of what is India today.

The standardization of the Acheulean handaxes over a wide geographic region (including Europe in later periods) and over nearly a million years of time supports the idea that *Homo erectus* possessed the intellectual ability to form a complex mental image of the form of the handaxe and this was transmitted culturally. In some circles of thought this standardization in toolmaking production also is seen as supporting the existence of language.

Genus *Homo* – *Homo heidelbergenesis*

The first permanent European colonization by humans occurred approximately 600,000 years ago. Although there is evidence of earlier human activity in Europe (at Sima del Elefante [Pit of the Elephant] in Atapuerca, Spain) at about 1.2 million years ago, the current thought is that these very early settlers died out. *Homo heidelbergenesis* brought the Acheulean handaxe technology to Europe and also likely brought sophisticated woodworking skills.

At a site known as Schoningen in what Germany is today we have an excellent preservation situation where several wooden throwing spears, with wooden tips, have been dated to approximately 300,000 years ago (Balter 2014a). Note the Schoningen dates have recently been modified, originally, they were thought to be older. These spears were carefully crafted, were delicately balanced, and resemble the size and proportions of modern javelins. As such they would have been excellent throwing weapons for big-game hunters. They also demonstrate a sophisticated knowledge of raw materials and the cognitive abilities necessary to intentionally produced them.

Homo heidelbergenesis is seen by many as a likely ancestor to the later Neanderthals although there is debate on whether or not this species should be considered a sub-species of *Homo erectus* (Balter 2014b).

Genus *Homo* – *Homo neanderthalensis*

First discovered and recognized in 1856, just a few years before Darwin's publication of the *Origin of the Species* (1859), the Neanderthals are named after the Neander Valley in what is today Germany where the first specimens were uncovered. They are aptly named because the translation of Neander Valley is literally "valley of the new man" and the Neanderthals were the first new species of humans ever discovered (Papagianni and Morse 2013).

Although there was great controversy at the time, which makes for fascinating reading, the Neanderthals were eventually recognized as a separate species of humans (in 1864). They are characterized by a generally robust postcranial skeleton (below the skull), large thick bones, a sloping forehead, a large bun-shaped occipital region (rear of the skull), heavy brow-ridges, and a brain size actually somewhat larger than modern humans.

The species is generally believed to date to about 150,000 years ago, although pre-Neanderthals have been identified as early as 300,000 years ago. Between about 48,000 and 30,000 years ago modern humans (Cro-Magnon) and Neanderthals co-existed in the eastern Mediterranean and Europe. For about 15,000 to 18,000 years these two human populations existed side by side until the Neanderthals eventually disappeared from their homeland in Europe between about 30,000 and 25,000 years ago.

There are those who view them as a subspecies of *Homo sapiens* rather than as a separate species. The debate is ongoing. For many years the Neanderthals were considered cousins, not ancestors, to modern humans but recent genetic research has shown that many modern human populations (except those of purely African descent) carry some Neanderthal genes (perhaps as much as 4 percent of their genome) (Sankararaman et. al 2014, Gibbons 2014, 2017). It is important to remember that Neanderthals evolved in Europe, not Africa, although their ancestors (and ours) likely originated in Africa.

That our human ancestors and Neanderthals from antiquity could, and did, interbreed, at least occasionally, raises a host of interesting questions. If we have Neanderthal genes in us then the Neanderthals were not our "cousins" but our ancestors. If your mother was a *Homo sapien* and your father was a Neanderthal, then what species are you? This fossil species concept based on morphology (bone structure) raises questions similar to those associated with the cultural concept of "race" based on different morphology (skin color largely) today (Cartmill 1999, Templeton 1999).

The biological definition of species says, generally, that if two species cannot interbreed and produce reproductively viable offspring, then they are separate species. However, in the fossil record we seldom can make this determination so the species definition is largely based on morphology (physical features) and this does not tell us if interbreeding is possible.

If the Neanderthals went extinct in Europe approximately 25,000 years ago but if a portion of their genome lives on in some of the human population then who is to say that, in some ways, the Neanderthals aren't still part of at least some of us? (Wynn 2012).

The Neanderthals were big-game hunters. A study comparing injuries sustained by Neanderthals and by rodeo riders shows a strong correlation in various types of skeletal injuries, particularly relating to the arms, pelvis, and feet. Modern rodeo riders have more head injuries than Neanderthals, but we can presume the Neanderthals were not riding their prey.

In stone tool technology, the Neanderthals were associated with the Mousterian industry which was much more complex than the earlier Acheulian industry. This industry utilized a fairly standardized production technique although the variety of flakes and toolkits (materials used for making the stone tools) varied widely.

Until recently there has been debate about whether the Neanderthals had speech or a engaged in complex symbolic behavior. While still unresolved recent discoveries and re-interpretations of existing evidence suggest that the Neanderthals, at least occasionally, buried their dead with associated artifacts like stone tools, produced rock art, and wore personal ornamentation. These are all characteristics of "modern human behavior" which I will discuss in more detail later.

Several lines of evidence support the notion that Neanderthals could speak. One is the hyoid bone in their skeletal remains. This bone is found in modern humans in the larynx region of the throat and is essential for speaking. Although only one complete Neanderthal hyoid bone has been discovered, its presence suggests some speech capability. The same line of reasoning that supports speech in earlier human populations such as *Homo erectus* and *Homo heidelbergenesis* based on standardized tool production can also be applied to Neanderthals. The debate is far from over. We also have what may be musical instruments associated with Neanderthals. A possible flute made of the femur of a young cave bear dating to approximately 45,000 years ago) was found in Slovenia in Eastern Europe. This and other evidence suggests to some that the Neanderthals may have had a richer and more varied cultural life than previously acknowledged (Hublin 2014, Mithen 2006).

Genus *Homo* – *Homo denisovan*

Recent finds (2010) in the Denisova Cave in southern Siberia have identified a heretofore unknown human species known as the Denisovans. Based on genetic analysis of a tooth and a small finger bone they date between 50,000 and 30,000 years ago. The genetic evidence suggests that they shared a common ancestry with the Neanderthals but were not Neanderthal. Traces of the Denisovan DNA survive in modern-day human populations in New Guinea and the Pacific Islands. This is a case of a human species being identified based on genetic evidence, not skeletal morphology, and a case of a newly discovered species that suggests there is much more to learn about human ancestry.

Genus *Homo* – *Homo floresiensis*

Otherwise known as the "Hobbit", *Homo floresiensis* was discovered in the Indonesian island of Flores in 2003 (Jacob et al. 2006). *Homo floresiensis* lived between about 95,000 and 17,000 years ago, (they disappeared after the Neanderthals disappeared). Individuals were fully bipedal and stood about 3 feet six inches tall and had small brains (about a third the size of modern humans) yet they made stone tools and hunted large rodents and small island elephants. So they were smaller than the australopithecines in body and somewhat similar in brain size but made stone tools. Like the Neanderthals, when they were first discovered great skepticism concerned their validity but overwhelming evidence quickly established *Homo floresiensis* as a new human species, one of several that have been discovered in the 21st century. Also, maybe this suggests that there is more to a brain than the size, perhaps there are other characteristics that we cannot see in the fossil record.

Genus *Homo* -- *Homo naledi*

In 2015 over 1,500 bones or bone fragments of a new hominin species was discovered nearly 100 feet underground in the Dinaledi Cave in South Africa. This species has many similarities to australopithecines (small body and small brain) but the hands and feet resemble living humans. No associated stone tools have been found. Current dates suggest that they are between 335,000 and 236,000 years old. Some think they may be a small-brained version of *Homo ergaster*. The bones are deposited in such a way, and without stone tool or carnivore marks, that suggest a type of cemetery deep underground. This is a provocative thought and, if true, will have profound implications concerning our understanding of ancestral hominin behavior. Research is ongoing (Klein 2018:104).

Redefining or Just Rethinking the Genus *Homo*

About 65 years ago there was fairly active debate in paleoanthropology (Tattersall 2000) about how the fossil record was being interpreted. Since then many new finds have contributed dramatically to our growing body of evidence. Many new finds are often assigned to a new species of *Homo* by their discoverers, often amongst great controversy. This has resulted in a plethora of human species, a few of which have been mentioned here. Genetic evidence of the past few years has demonstrated that at least three "species" could interbreed, the Neanderthals, the Denisovans, and *Homo sapiens*.

This has led some to reconsider the earlier debates and suggests that perhaps these species are more a figment of our modern imagination (based on physical characteristics) than actual distinct species. If humans can adapt to any ecosystem due to culture (discussed earlier) and interbreed then speciation within the human lineage is arguably technically impossible (Ackerman and Smith 2007, Bruner 2004, Brauer 2008, Dobzhansky 1944, 1962, 1963, Groves 2004, Mellars 2005). If so, then we are left with a wide variety of related specimens (but not species) reflecting a rich diversity of physical structure, but which are all related. This is not the prevailing view in paleoanthropology but it is worth perhaps reconsidering (DeSalle and Tattersall 2008, Gibbons 2015).

In a sense this simplifies the "family tree" and generally leaves us with modern human varieties (less than 200,000 years old), ancestral human varieties (between 200,000 and 1.6 million years ago), and formative human varieties (over 1.6 million years ago). The date ranges are mine alone based on the dates mentioned above. The debate continues and probably will not be resolved soon.

Anatomically Modern Humans

Anatomically Modern Humans (AMH) first appear in the fossil record approximately 200,000 years ago. There is some debate about this and some suggest the date is more recent, perhaps 100,000 years ago. At this point in time the evidence is limited to the morphological characteristics of the available hominin fossils.

Modern Human Behavior

If AMH appeared 200,000 years ago then Modern Human Behavior (MHB) seems to have developed over a long period, perhaps 100,000 years or more. There has been considerable debate on whether it appeared in a flash, as if a lightbulb was turned on, or if it developed more slowly. The growing consensus, if there is one, is that it developed in fits and starts, appearing in one region but not continuing, then appearing in another region, and so forth until at some point it reached the "critical mass" of population necessary for long-term continuity, which would (of course) be culturally transmitted.

Indicators of modern human behavior in the archaeological record include symbolic representation which is often characterized by art and by personal ornamentation. It is thought that fully articulate speech was necessary for this process to occur. Some of the earliest examples of artwork (symbolism) date to about 75,000 years ago. A well-known example is the incised markings on a small piece of red ocher from the Blombos Cave in South Africa (Marean 2007). There is a saying, "EARTH without ART is "EH". The material record might support this in great antiquity.

Other characteristics of modern human behavior that are important include sophisticated hunting methods and much more complex stone toolmaking technologies

Art and Technology in Pleistocene Europe

AMH arrived in Europe approximately 48,000 years ago and developed a rich tradition of art including the intricate painting of the interior of some cave walls, sculpture, the decoration of portable objects, and personal adornment.

The reasons behind this explosion in creativity are much debated but the skill, craftsmanship and cognitive ability they represent are beyond question today, although in the late 1800's when they were first discovered and before their antiquity was recognized there was much controversy (Curtis 2006).

The original Paleolithic cave art discovery was at Altamira, Spain and the discoverer was accused of forging the images on the cave walls. Scholars of the time could not believe that something that old could be so well designed and executed.

It was originally believed that "primitive art" slowly evolved from simple geometric forms and shapes and eventually reached its peak toward the end of the Ice Age. Recent discoveries dating to the mid 1990's at places like Grotte de Chauvet, France (dating to about 32,000 years ago) have turned this idea on its head (Chauvet 1996). Some of the oldest cave paintings are some of the most visually complex and the creators utilized techniques such as perspective and stump drawing (basically varying the size of lines) not seen again until the rise of the Renaissance masters. Some interpretations of key complex imagery suggest that the illusion of movement (in flickering torchlight) was possible, perhaps making this the earliest moving picture.

The interior of these dark caves were usually sealed by a natural rock fall tens of thousands of years ago and contains complex polychromatic (multicolor) images that clearly were pre-planned. The pigments, layout and positioning of the images was not accidental and, in some cases, (Lascaux is an example) large quantities of charcoal pigment had to be brought in.

The interior of the caves where the artwork is found were usually completely dark and, contrary to popular belief, were not used for habitation and occupation, except perhaps by dangerous cave bears. The places were visited and decorated intentionally and apparently intermittently, with perhaps thousands of years between visits, which suggests a long degree of temporal cultural continuity.

Remember, the humans who created these images were mobile hunter-gatherers who ranged widely over the landscape and did not remain in one place very long. The images they created show a detailed knowledge of the natural environment and a particularly acute awareness of the proportions of the creatures they shared the landscape with, and suggests that they revisited special places, at least periodically. More on this later.

The imagery is largely representational although some abstract and geometric forms exist. There are also very few images of humans in the galleries (although some apparently discarded sketch-slates exist which suggest relatively short hairstyles, for one example) (Curtis 2006). It is almost as if the artists considered themselves to be secondary to the main players who were mastodons, rhinos, horse, bison, reindeer, and other wild (by our definition) animals, including birds. Interestingly, not all of the animals portrayed on the cave walls were regularly consumed as prey.

Another aspect of the cave art is the hand prints. By mixing colored ochre (usually red) with a binder of some type, perhaps water or saliva, the artist would blow a mouthful of colored pigment through a hollow tube over his or her hand and leave a negative hand imprint on the wall of the cave. Because these binders and pigments are sometimes organic, they can often be dated through radiocarbon techniques.

In one particular cave an artist deep in prehistory had a crooked little finger on one hand, and his or her ventures throughout the interior of the dark cave can be traced by the unique hand prints left behind. We also have immature human footprints in the caves, and tracks left by canines. We do not know if these were domesticated canines or not. If so then we have the earliest evidence of perhaps a "boy and his dog" domestication by humans, at about 32,000 years ago although some studies suggest a much earlier date for dog domestication, perhaps as early as 135,000 years ago) (Herzog 2010, Grimm 2015).

Some handprints show missing digits or portions of digits. Early thought was that the creators had suffered the loss of digits due perhaps to accidents or injury. Another view is that they were intentionally made by bending fingers to form hand signs of some type. If so then we have the earliest evidence of nonverbal communication through hand signaling, much like modern signing used by deaf individuals, and even perhaps by hunters. As drivers of cars, we are all familiar with the meaning of intentional hand signals today. Unfortunately we cannot decipher these signals, or many other early writings (discussed below) (Guthrie 2005).

Not all of the artwork created by early humans was permanently fixed to the cave walls. We have intricately carved portable items including the famous "Venus" figurines, delicate flutes made from bird bones and mammoth ivory, decorated utilitarian items such as spear throwers (atlatls), hollow carved stone lamps that would have held fat and a wick for lighting, clay sculptures, and perhaps most famously of all, carved images of mythical beings that are half human and half animal.

The Hohlenstein-Stadel figurine is an excellent example It dates to about 40,000 years ago and is an intricately carved image with a human body and the head of a lion. Known as a theri-anthropomorphic image, this is one of the earliest known examples of figurative art. The intentional creation of a hybrid creature suggests that a complex cognitive thought process and a rich repertoire of abstract symbolic communication was well established by this time in prehistory (Wynn and Bright 2009).

The stone toolmaking technology of Europe during this time period indicates an increasing specialization. Whether the toolkits represent different culture groups or different activities by the same prehistoric cultures is largely unresolved (Binford 1966). As time progressed the stone tools became smaller and many were mounted in antler, bone, or possibly wooden handles to serve as many specialized tools. These are composite tools because they were made of more than one material. The culture periods of Pleistocene Europe associated with AMH, from oldest to most recent are largely defined by their stone tools and the complexity of them.

Europe is not alone in the rich collection of symbolic imagery and art reaching deep into prehistory. Some of the rock art in Australia may be as old, or older, than the painted caves of Europe and deserves more careful attention, if the descendent population should agree.

The Dispersal (Our Great Migrations)

We do not know if Anatomically Modern Humans originated in Africa and migrated to other regions of the world and then replaced the descendants of *Homo erectus* (or other undiscovered species) or if local populations of *Homo erectus* independently evolved into AMH.

There are two competing hypotheses about this. One is the multiregional hypothesis which proposes that AMH developed independently in Africa, Europe, and Asia. This theory suggests that the biological diversity of contemporary humans in different regions has deep roots in prehistory and is based largely on physical characteristics.

The Out-of-Africa hypothesis proposes that AMH evolved in tropical Africa before about 150,000 years ago then migrated into other parts of the world and replaced the indigenous populations of earlier human species. Some evidence suggests a single movement out of Africa perhaps about 83,000 years ago. Other evidence suggests two exits from Africa into Southwest Asia and beyond. The first exit occurred sometime after approximately 100,000 years ago, and the second perhaps as recently as 70,000 years ago. Both migrations would likely have involved small groups of breeding populations.

As I said earlier, if we set aside our preoccupation with species as defined through physical features in the fossil record (morphology) and accept that a species whose main adaptive strategy is through culture (not tooth and fang) then the idea of genetically distinct species of humans becomes less important, particularly after about 200,000 years ago.

There is a third option, which is a combination of the two competing hypotheses, which allows for some interbreeding between AMH and other earlier species. This is supported by the genetic evidence that both Neanderthal and Denisovan DNA in modern human populations.

The first AMH migration out of Africa apparently reached Southwestern Asia about 100,000 years ago. These individuals co-existed alongside Neanderthals in the region for about 20,000 years before the Neanderthals became extinct. This is not the only known group of isolated modern human populations to disappear, isolated island populations off the coast of Australia have been witness to human populations cut off from the mainland when the sea levels rose following the end of the last glaciation, ending in their local extinction..

Modern humans had permanently settled in Southwestern Asia by about 50,000 years ago. By about 48,000 years ago modern humans had reached Eastern Europe (and met the indigenous Neanderthal population). By about 30,000 years ago modern humans were in Eastern Asia and Siberia. During this time, the glaciers covered most of the polar regions and the settlers in Europe and eastern Asia faced both short and long-term climatic shifts from bitter cold to somewhat warmer conditions. The extreme northeast portion of Asia seems to have been devoid of human settlement until much later.

By about 45,000 years ago or humans had reached Australia. This was during the last ice age when the sea levels were approximately 300 (or more) feet lower than today. At this time, New Guinea and Australia formed a single landmass called Sahul, and many islands of Southeast Asia were also connected by another landmass called Sundaland.

Even with the lower sea level in order to reach Australia from Sundaland (or the islands of what is now Indonesia) it would have been necessary to cross the Wallacea Straight. This implies that breeding populations (not a bunch of men on a raft fishing) of humans likely reached Australia because of deliberate sea voyaging. If this is true we have evidence that humans were using open-water craft in the southwestern Pacific about 30,000 years ago. Traveling by boat, it seems, is could be a very, very old human practice.

By approximately 20,000 to 15,000 years ago (most say 18,000 years ago) modern humans had reached North America most likely from northeastern Siberia across the Bering land bridge (known as Beringia) into what is today Alaska. At the time the sea levels were low enough for hunting groups to cross between continents on foot without likely knowing they were doing so. Eventually the polar ice sheets melted and North America became separated from eastern Asia.

There is no direct archaeological evidence of earlier human settlement in the Americas, or by other bipedal hominins (such as the mythical "bigfoot"). At this time, it appears that the entire continent was originally populated solely by *Homo sapiens*. Research is ongoing.

The Bearing land bridge was last submerged under the rising sea about 11,000 years ago. At the time it was a treeless arctic environment with various types of vegetation. Crossing it on foot would have required no special new skills. An alternate theory suggests that the Americas may have been populated along a coastal route using small watercraft (perhaps prototypes of kayaks) and breeding populations of humans hunting mammals and fish in a coastal marine environment. The two migration theories are not mutually exclusive, it could have occurred by one method, or the other, or both.

The oldest well-dated people in North America are the Clovis people who date to about 13,200 years ago. But one of the oldest archaeological sites in the Americas is Monte Verde (likely a campsite) which is in what is today southern Chili and which apparently predates the Clovis culture, or is at least roughly in the same time period. It is perplexing why one of the oldest archaeological sites in Americas lies at the southern extreme of the continent if the original inhabitants came across the north. This suggests that perhaps a maritime route along the Pacific coast may have aided in the overland colonization or that perhaps there are many more sites to find, or both.

Several lines of evidence support a migration from Asia to the Americas. One is the dental similarities between northern Asian populations and Native Americans. Dental features such as incisor shoveling, single-rooted upper first premolars and triple-rooted lower first molars are good examples. This is known as sinodontic evidence.

Genetic and linguistic evidence also supports a migration from Asia and suggests there may have been several migratory episodes over the several thousands of years that the Bering land bridge was open. The earliest documented inhabitants of the Americas (the Clovis people mentioned earlier), were big-game hunters who expanded across North America in almost a "blitzkrieg" fashion in a mere 300 years. They flourished between 13,200 and 12,900 years ago although there is a growing body of evidence of an earlier sparse pre-Clovis occupation.

After about 12,000 years ago shortly following the arrival of *Homo sapiens* in the Americas, many species of Pleistocene animals (most but not all were very large) became extinct, including the mammoth, mastodon, horse, and large bison of antiquity (Martin 1984). There is controversy about whether human exploitation contributed to this mass extinction or it was a part of a larger sequence of relatively swift environmental changes that many native species could not adapt to at the end of the last Ice Age. This debate, like so many others, is ongoing.

THE LONG WALK HERE

5 HUNTING AND GATHERING

First let us set aside pretty much everything we think we know about the hunting-gathering lifestyle. Set aside the preconception that life was "nasty, brutish, and short" also set aside the preconception they were "noble savages" living in harmony with their environment. Both are correct and both are wrong (LeBlanc 2003).

The fact is humanity spent almost 99% of its time on this planet as hunter-gatherers. We evolved this way. Bipedalism and toolmaking are a large part of this. So is being a social creature. And the two may be related. It is complex but some evidence suggests that toolmaking and language may have developed together.

Anthropologists can study modern hunter-gatherers (of which there are very few) but it is a challenge to extrapolate back in time based solely on this data (this is called ethnographic analogy). Modern hunter-gatherers that we study all know and have been in contact with sedentary agricultural groups missionaries, government authorities, and anthropologists for centuries and so they differ from what their ancestors probably were like in terms of extracting resources (Wobst 1978).

One thing about hunting and gathering we have learned is that is more like gathering than hunting. Studies have shown that gathering wild nuts, berries, plants, and small animals garners more calories, day-to-day, than the "big hunt". We think of hunter-gatherers as nomadic people, and most are, but there are also sedentary and semi-sedentary hunter-gatherers. Often these should be called fisher-gatherers because they are usually strategically located to take seasonal advantage of extremely productive marine resources, such as the salmon runs in the Pacific Northwest (Arnold 1992).

Another thing about hunter-gatherers to set aside is the concept they were an egalitarian society. Yes, there is little if any formal status differentiation overall. But hunter-gatherers self-segregate just like any human group; largely based on age, sex, or affiliation through blood or clan or both. A more useful definition is "acephalous" meaning that their group leaders were temporary and leadership was largely based on skill.

Theirs was largely what we have come to call a meritocracy not an autocracy (one leader for everything - which is a modern state concept) (Sahlins 1972(1998), Shepard 1992, Gowdy 1998, Yellen 1989, Woodburn 1981, Zerzan 1994). Leaders served on an ad-hoc or just-in-time basis for generally one thing due to their skills and ability in an economy that depended on immediate returns for a particular goal. It was not until the advent of agriculture that we begin to see delayed-return labor systems and long-term storage, and long-term leaders, generally. In a well-stated carton, we (as hunter-gatherers) just need enough to get by until we need more (Hoest 2017). That is the way we lived for nearly 99% of our time on this planet. I would be shocked if there is not a genetic component to this, but that is for another work by someone smarter than me.

We rarely find elite prestige goods in hunter-gatherer burials, when we find hunter-gatherer burials at all (and cemeteries [villages for the dead] are something that sedentary societies invented). We do not find such prestige goods associated with infants or children. It is only with the advent of agriculture and class distinction that exotic materials and prestige items become part of the burial assemblage for infants. We find interesting decorative and perhaps even sacred items associated with hunter-gatherer burials, but only intermittently.

Most hunter-gatherers were mobile, moving from base camp to base camp throughout the year in something we call a seasonal round (no they did not wander randomly through the landscape, think back to *Homo erectus*) in a pattern that is sometimes called "transhumance", see Kelly 1983). Sometimes they disaggregated into smaller groups seasonally and fanned out over the landscape, and then later re-aggregated into larger groups annually (temporarily) to accomplish many things, including finding mates, trading goods, and visiting with distant relatives and kin.

Such gatherings were usually accompanied by a feast that included days and days of singing, dancing, the consumption of large amounts of food, and perhaps most important ... storytelling and re-enacting important events in the shared memory (mythology) of the group (Cron 2012, Gottschall 2012, Hayden 2011, Simmons 2007). Also, contrary to popular belief hunter-gatherers did not live year-round in caves, they constructed short term structures (often called wickiups) even if they were staying someplace for just one or two nights (Martin 2016).

If you are a mobile society then the accumulation of material items can only make mobility more difficult. Hunter-gatherers use, modify, and discard things. Most things that we find in the archaeological record are stone tools. When they were finished with something like a worn-out stone scraper that can't be further modified (Blades 2003) they typically dropped it and forgot about it before it hit the ground, much like a child today might carelessly drop an aluminum chewing gum wrapper while walking through the park. By the way, I am glad they did that, because it left a record for us. In my class I often have students study a park, and look for little clues that can tell us about human activity in the park.

Hunter-gatherers were not hoarders although they cached useful items (like stone spear points) in secure locations to be retrieved later, perhaps next season, when they returned in their seasonal rounds. Hunter-gatherers were also not terribly frugal. We have evidence of mass killings of herd animals (by running an entire herd off a cliff for example) then the select removal of only some of the meat. This is called "gourmet butchering". Before judging them, remember the dangers associated with hunting large animals and the lack of storage or the ability to carry large amounts of meat from one location to another.

Hunter-gatherers lived in what we typically call a Stone Age technology. They did not develop complex metalworking although when available they sometimes made use of copper, bronze and iron (in later periods). By working suitable stone and volcanic glass (obsidian) they were able to make extremely sharp and useful tools. They also fashioned materials out of bone and wood. They did not cultivate and tend plants in gardens or fields, but there is a growing body of evidence that they were thoroughly familiar with the available plant species and took advantage of more of them then we do today.

Stone tool technology is much, much, more than simply smashing two rocks together to see what happens. It is a deliberate reduction technology, much like sculpting. First you must find the right materials. Not just any rock will do, you need something that will fracture in a controlled fashion and hold its form under duress. Typically we find such stone tools made of various types of chert (or other cryptocrystalline rocks) and obsidian (which is a volcanic glass), although a wide variety of materials were used. When a good source was located the area was quarried, often for centuries. Hunter-gatherers were the original miners and evidence of their strategic quarrying activities is with us today.

When you consider that source materials have a distinctive chemical signature due to the geologic nature of their original formation it is possible to trace the distribution of those materials across the landscape. It is evident because of studies of source materials that hunter-gatherers either traveled over vast territories or were engaged in complex down-the-line trading networks, or both.

Back to stone toolmaking. Until the modern laser-scalpel, obsidian (volcanic glass) was the sharpest blade ever produced. It is much sharper than a steel blade. Electron microscope imaging has demonstrated that obsidian blades are so sharp they can push the cells of plant or animal material apart, instead of jaggedly tearing them in two like a razor blade might do. This handiwork is much too fine for the naked eye to see although I have cut myself enough times with obsidian (when flintknapping) and with razor blades (when cleaning fryers in a fast-food restaurant in high school) to know that a fine obsidian cut will heal much faster, and with a much smaller scar, than a razor blade cut.

The final product of stone toolmaking (often called flint knapping) is something with a pre-determined shape. This takes us back to the sculpting analogy I made earlier. The stone toolmaker must know his/her material and must have a pre-conceived idea of what they were trying to create. It is a complex process but once you master it, it is replicable. There is evidence that flintknapping might have been a specialty activity and if so then it suggests that not all hunter-gatherers were also flintknappers. This supports the notion of craft specialization in a pre-agricultural setting. We know from the remains of the flintknapping process that not all knappers were right handed. Apparently something close to the same distribution of left handedness and right handedness existed in prehistory as today.

So we have established that hunter-gatherers are a Stone Age people (typically called Paleolithic) who mined suitable materials for pre-determined purposes, who took advantage of a wide variety of plant and animal resources in their environment, who (mostly) traveled through their environment in a seasonal fashion taking advantage of resources in different locals at different times of the year. They also worked in wood and bone. Theirs was a complex existence although they did so with no sort of hereditary leadership. They did not cultivate plants or animals, although there is evidence they did perhaps domesticate the dog somewhere between about 135,000 and 32,000 years ago. This is much longer ago than any plant or any other animal domestication,

Hunter-gatherers also made things out of clay. Sometimes they fired the clay items. Usually these items appear to be images of animals but sometimes they are geometric in shape. Depending on the part of the world you are investigating you might also find human images. So they understood how to make things out of clay but they did not make pottery, why? One reason many (but not all) hunter-gatherer groups did not appear to utilize pottery is that it is so easily breakable. If you are moving across the landscape regularly (on your own two feet), pottery is both heavy and fragile. Imagine carrying a terra cotta flower pot on your daily three-mile walk to collect food items. A simple wicker basket might work much better.

How then, does one boil water if you do not have pottery? There are many ways to do this but one typical method involves creating a container made of skin or some other animal part (like a stomach) to hold water. Suspend it in a tripod and drop red-hot rocks from a fire into it until it heats up. The rocks will crack and fracture when they hit the cold water and this may explain why we find so much fire cracked rock in hunter-gatherer sites.

Hunter-gatherers also could apparently live to a ripe old age. Some skeletal evidence suggests late 60's or early 70's was possible. This presumes that one did not die of an injury (broken bone) or disease (usually some intestinal parasite due to drinking contaminated water or eating infested meat). Hunter-gatherers did not have emergency rooms and if you suffered a debilitating injury and the camp moved on, you were likely left to die alone.

This gets us to the question of social organization. Hunter-gatherer groups were typically very small. Usually fewer than 100 and sometimes much smaller family-based units that would seasonally aggregate then disaggregate over the landscape.

Evidence suggests that seasonal rounds throughout a known environment was the basis of their food procurement strategy. In the summer, they would camp in one area, another in the fall, another in the winter, and another in the spring. Often camps moved more frequently than every few months and sometimes they were apparently stationery for longer periods. While we may not know the exact year of a prehistoric hunter-gatherer site we can deduce the season in which it was occupied by the plants and ages of animals harvested.

A good example is a site with young deer bones. Hunter-gatherers did not have storage (mostly) so when we find a large grouping of young deer bones we know that the site was likely being occupied in the spring. The same applies to various types of plant remains. It is paradoxical that the evidence can tell us the season but not the exact year.

Hunter-gatherers also apparently did not engage in warfare, at least not organized warfare as we know it. Archaeological evidence speaks to the existence of conflict and occasionally death at the hands of another human (with a stone tipped spear), but by and large hunter-gatherers seem to have avoided violent confrontation and instead chose to splinter-off (a budding process) and move to other unoccupied areas, when conflict arose. As time went on and populations grew there were fewer and fewer options like this that were available.

Revenge killings are a different thing. In today's world if someone murders somebody else the state takes over and imposes sanctions. In a world where there are no leaders and no prisons, there is no such option. If a killing occurred, and this is based on relatively recent ethnographical evidence, then compensation was due. The question of fault was apparently largely irrelevant. The question of the morality of taking a human life was apparently largely irrelevant. The question of compensation and restitution was apparently key.

If the family of the murderer failed to make restitution to the family of the victim, regardless of the circumstances of the conflict, then any member of the murder's family was fair game for a revenge killing if the actual murderer could not be found. This perpetuated an endless cycle of violence that appears small-scale but when you consider the small size of the groups involved it quickly becomes apparent that a "Hatfield-McCoy" feud is not sustainable. Sooner or later one group will lose one too many productive members and will cease to exist (see Diamond 2013 for more on this in village life).

One group could also ambush another group and annihilate them. The evidence suggests this may have been more common than previously thought although young women and sometimes very young boys may have been spared an assimilated into the conquering group. There is evidence there could have also been a differentiation in social status in hunter-gatherers based on the way you joined the group.

This behavior is characteristic of any society (agricultural included) where traditional tribal affiliations are important to individual and group identity. When a member of your group is injured by a member of another group, then any member of the other group becomes a potential revenge target, regardless of their "individual" involvement, age, sex, or status. Often, societal elders play an important role in fanning or in mediating these disputes.

Usually warfare apparently consisted of intergroup skirmishes that might involve a few casualties and a repeated cycle of revenge killings and then more conflict as the opportunity presented itself. The evidence on this is not conclusive and may be conflated (mixed) with ethnographic details about essentially Neolithic (new stone age) agricultural groups. Hunter-gatherers did apparently raid other groups and kidnap potential brides and/or make symbolic "coup" killings or taking body parts (such as scalps) as trophies that did not necessarily kill the victim. The evidence is mostly recent (a few hundred years of observation) and is very difficult to unravel.

One thing is clear. Hunter-gatherers did not have institutions like hospitals with emergency rooms, jails, or prisons, or cemeteries. These came later with settled agriculturalists. Situations were dealt with on the spot (or in modern economic terms "just in time").

Hunter-gatherer spirituality or cosmology apparently reflected little in terms of established human social institutions and hierarchies of human-like gods. The vast majority of Upper Paleolithic art in Europe and also more recent studies in North America suggests that hunter-gatherers were focused on the natural environment. Their religions were "naturalistic" ones that focused on the animals. When you consider that your group travels through the landscape in search of seasonally available plant and animal resources this makes sense.

Very few images of human actors are evident in early hunter-gatherer art motifs. Most of the imagery is about the natural resources that were available. Think of it as a catalogue of what is available in the supermarket. Yes this is a crude analogy but any modern picker-packer knows exactly where the choice items are in their favorite store just as their hunter-gatherer ancestors did before them.

We typically call hunter-gatherer religion shamanistic. The term shaman is used so often that it is almost without meaning. For general consideration think of a shaman as an individual with a special relationship with the supernatural. What the supernatural is, is largely irrelevant. The shaman is the conduit to another place or dimension, perhaps a place where healing can occur and perhaps a place where one can find a vision that will lead you to something important like your animal spirit-guide, or maybe just to good hunting. Maybe the shaman is not a shaman, but is instead a sorcerer (not a healer), and will use his/her powers to bring harm to someone, one must be careful.

How does the shaman acquire this special relationship? Perhaps it is through training (again evidence of early craft specialization), or perhaps it is by disposition/personality, or perhaps through hallucinogenic substances. Yes the archaeological record supports the concept that our ancestors knew of the mind-altering properties of certain plant materials, and of certain experiences such as fasting and sensory deprivation. We have evidence of shamanistic-like traditions worldwide, and the one thing they all seem to have in common is that they are more naturalistic in orientation than most modern religions.

In his famous piece on hunter-gatherers *The Original Affluent Society* (1972) Marshall Sahlins makes several points. One of them is that hunter-gatherers seem to have been able to work an incredibly short work week by modern standards. In just a few hours a day one person could gather enough protein and carbohydrates to sustain three people in his/her band for several days.

When you add in the largesse of a successful (if intermittent) hunting expedition the results in terms of subsistence are really prolific. Of course the environment is unpredictable and sometimes the results of a day's activity are good and sometimes not good. Hunter-gatherers seem, by this metric, to lead a life of feast and famine. The advantage that hunger-gatherers always had over agriculturists is the ability to move from one area to another better area, as the resource availability changed. In drought situations some agricultural communities in modern Africa have been known to temporarily "hang out" with their neighboring hunger-gatherer friends to survive.

Everyone has nothing or everyone has something. Sometimes the something is more than enough. One person can support three, although apparently, they take turns, and nobody works more than what comes down to about 3-5 "ish" hours a day (Bird David 1992, Lee 1968).

Of course there issues about the definition of work, for example does that include food preparation? Who does the dishes? Oh, there are no hunter-gatherer dishes. There are also other issues such as sharing. Some have suggested that hunter-gatherers were so entirely co-dependent that by today's standards they could be diagnosed with the psychological disorder co-dependency (under the American Psychological Association guidelines). There was apparently no room for anyone to stash or hoard their share of the group's daily food harvest, and anybody who did so was subject to social criticism and possibly the worst punishment ... ostracism.

What all this means for modern humans is enough to write a book on. We have briefly discussed mobility, technology, social relations, and cosmology, to name just a few items.

Just take walking for example. If hunter-gatherers walked an average of 5K (three miles) every three days (that is what archaeologists call a catchment area) then they are walking at least three 5Ks a week. How many modern humans sitting at a desk do that much sustained walking in a week?

What about our ancestors' tendency to gorge themselves when food was available so they had enough body fat to sustain themselves when food was scarce (something called the thrifty gene hypothesis) (Hales and Barker 2001, Neel 1962). How does this relate to our inherited ability to store body fat in an environment when there is no food scarcity or much walking? What does this tell us about ways to possibly treat and maybe prevent obesity and diabetes?

The list goes on, and on, and on. What about salt in our diets? What about the necessary amino acids? What about sweets and glycerin to fuel brain activity? What about our possibly 32,000-year relationship with dogs? Apparently, they are the only other species of animal on this planet that actually "likes" us and may have co-evolved with us. Cats are a different matter. Reflect on this and see how complex the questions become.

What about the majesty of existing in the living interactive theater of nature where everything has a place that does not need us to function? How do we find or define ourselves in such a place? Perhaps the entire modern concept of "self" and the 20th century Jungian concept of "personality" needs to be re-explored in this light. They seem to have done just fine without it.

In this section I have challenged you to think about the hunter-gatherer lifestyle a little more deeply. This represents almost 99% of our time on this planet as humans, although admittedly most humans who ever lived did so in the realm of agriculture, settled existence, ownership, storage, delayed return activities, hierarchical religions, prestige goods, and inherited status.

By the beginning of the Holocene it is estimated there were only about 8.5 million people in the world, all hunter-gatherers. So, all of our ancestors were hunter-gatherers, for a long, long time. And they walked a lot.

The rest of this book takes us through that journey, region by region into pre-industrial agriculture and early states. At the end I will come back and discuss some implications of this about our lives today.

6 AFTER THE ICE MELTED

About 15,000 BCE the glaciers were at their maximum extent (in the northern hemisphere) then something dramatic happened to the climate of earth. It warmed up. This marks the end of a geological epoch called the Pleistocene and the beginning of the Holocene. This didn't happen all at once. Things started warming up about 13,700 BCE then the warming trend reversed itself and for nearly a thousand years and the climate returned to near-glacial conditions (from about 10,950 BCE to about 9,500 BCE). This cold snap is called the Younger Dryas, and it is important for reasons I will explain later.

After the Younger Dryas the warming trend we are in today began in earnest. It affected different regions of the world differently, depending largely on the geography and the latitude (proximity to the polar ice caps). So, by about 11,000 years ago we had firmly entered the Holocene epoch and this is when we see great changes, including agriculture.

This was not the first time that near-global glacial conditions were interrupted with a warm period. Over the last several million years there has been a cycle of long glacial periods interrupted by shorter warm spells. We are in one such natural warm spell right now (although it appears to be getting warmer faster than in previous interglacials and has the potential to out-warm them).

When the ice melted there were regional and local changes in vegetation and in the mammals that grazed on the vegetation. Sea levels rose dramatically (by several hundred feet or more) and there was regional flooding as the ice sheets of the northern latitudes melted. Some of these ice sheets were as thick as a mile.

It also marked the end of what we know as the Paleolithic period and the beginning of something called the Mesolithic, or in some circles the Epipaleolithic. This ultimately led to the Neolithic (and associated plant and animal domestication - agriculture) in many regions of the world.

Imagine a scenario where hunter-gatherers who existed on a limited supply of megafauna saw their traditional prey disappear and smaller (but still large) animals increased in population and take over new environmental niches. For example, in North America many species of Ice Age animals became extinct by about 11,000 BCE (mentioned earlier). Imagine an increase in the quantity of a wide variety of plant species and new microenvironments that could be exploited. Combine this with a slow but dramatic increase in the human population, which had been relatively stable for tens of thousands of years and you might think you were living in a "Garden of Eden"

After a couple thousand years of warming the human population increased and there were fewer prime unoccupied areas to move into, then something else dramatic happened. It got cold again, very cold, and very fast. The earth rapidly returned to near-glacial conditions. This "cold snap" is called the Younger Dryas (mentioned earlier) and it lasted for nearly a millennium. This is a critical event because it is thought by many it may have provided the impetus for humans to plant and harvest wild cereals and grains and to corral and eventually domesticate many herd animals.

What this leads to is a question of some importance. Was plant and animal domestication an invention or a strategy? If it was an invention, then it was likely desirable and led to leisure time (for some) that allowed a few people to specialize in various crafts and occupations. If it was a strategy then it was something that hunter-gatherers reluctantly adopted in response to changing environmental conditions and associated population pressures. It is worth noting that in the historical record most hunter-gatherer populations avidly resisted forceful settlement and the adoption of agriculture.

As things warmed up (but before the cold snap) hunter-gatherer societies throughout the world developed new local methods of adapting to the changing environment. Overall the general trend was that the stone tools became smaller and more specialized. Large thrusting spears were replaced by the atlatl (a dart with a throwing stick for leverage) and later the bow and arrow which were more suitable for hunting smaller game (Peterson 1998). But do not forget that game can be hunted in other ways too, including using nets, bolas, sling shots (which are all difficult to find in the archaeological record) and by running entire herds off cliffs or into marshes or box canyons.

Highly mobile hunter-gatherers engaged largely in foraging for most of the Paleolithic but by the Mesolithic (or Epipaleolithic) we see an increase in intentional collecting and sometimes the appearance of limited storage and semi-sedentary settlement patterns. Foragers set up a base camp and move it frequently when local resources are depleted. Food is gathered daily. Collectors move camp less frequently and can engage in more intensive and broad-spectrum exploitation of local resources, sometimes with limited storage capabilities at the longer-term base camp. Collectors also require a more complex set of social rules to redistribute the accumulated and stored food.

The typical catchment area for hunter-gatherers is about a hour walk from base camp (roughly 5 kilometers or approximately 3 miles, sometimes more). For farming communities, the catchment area is typically much less than that.

With collectors, we see a more intensive exploitation of the environment and more of a "broad spectrum" adaptation to the environment. An example in northwestern Europe is the relatively fast disappearance of Magdalenian and other late Ice Age cultures who hunted reindeer on the open tundra with the appearance of forest and coastal hunting-and gathering practices. Hunter-gatherers also harvested and processed a wide variety of vegetable foods. We find specialized stone pounders and grinders used for processing plants during this period. It is generally believed that the European Mesolithic period represents a transition from glacial to post-glacial environments by the indigenous population.

We also see examples of more long-distance exchange and evidence of the appearance of social ranking detected in the presence of burial ornaments for some but not most individuals. This means that social ranking may have predated the adoption of agriculture, at least in some areas. Overall the archaeological record of the world between about 13,000 BCE and about 5,000 BCE shows a trend toward greater complexity in hunter-gatherer societies. After the adoption of early forms of agriculture in some areas by about 10,000 BCE (Scarre 2013b) we see greater interdependence, more long-distance exchange of raw materials (perhaps due to the necessities of sedentism), the emergence of an elite class, and ever increasing social complexity; due perhaps to the larger population of the time.

A good example from the eastern Mediterranean is the Natufian culture. They occupied a region that later become the western portion (or "hook") of the Fertile Crescent (see next chapter), otherwise known as the Levant. The Natufians were intensive foragers of wild cereals and nuts. They also hunted gazelles. The Natufians were semi-sedentary hunter-gatherers and perhaps were preadapted to eventually adopting agriculture and domesticating animals and settling down into a sedentary lifestyle (Bar-Yosef 1998).

Robert Braidwood's Hilly Flanks Hypothesis (in Scarre 2013) suggests that as the forests and dense woodland environments expanded in the eastern Mediterranean after the Holocene the local Natufian population expanded. With the onset of the Younger Dryas and the disappearance of wild wheats and ryes on the outskirts of the wooded areas the Natufians are thought to have begun to intentionally plant and harvest wild seeds as a survival strategy that continued after the return to warmer conditions.

This may have led, through artificial selection, to the appearance of domesticated wheat and rye in the region. What I have presented here is an oversimplified scenario but it should demonstrate how agriculture could have originated not so much as an "invention" but as an "strategy" for coping with a changing environment. We see Natufian sickles with obsidian blades embedded in jaw bones for harvesting wild grains and we see Natufian mortars and pestles for grinding plant materials in the archaeological record. We also see Natufian house foundations in what is today Jordan, that suggests a more sedentary lifestyle. The city of Jericho was built on the site of a Natufian camp located near a natural spring.

Other early hypotheses about the origins of agriculture include V. Gordon Childe's concept of a "Neolithic Revolution" (Childe 1971) that occurred in Southwest Asia during a period of severe drought. In more recent years the concept of an agricultural revolution has largely been replaced by thoughts about a more gradual transition.

There are many theories about the origins of food production. Some theories focus on population pressures (Cohen 1977), some on social forces (Bender 1981), others on population and resources (Smith 1998), some on ecological considerations (Flannery 1972), some on social competition (Hayden 2003 and Flannery 1972), and some on climate change (Braidwood 1983). The key here is that most theories today recognize that the answer probably lies in a multivariate approach where numerous factors come into play at different times and in different places. No one theory or school of thought seems to fit all the examples of the transformation to agricultural production around the world through time, although forced sedentism and population pressure seem to have a common role.

Generally speaking, the development of new food-producing economies took place in two steps. The first saw sowing and harvesting of wild plants and some control over locally available herd animals. Most of the diet seems to have still been from game and wild vegetable foods. By about 8750 BCE (Fagan 2007:212) in southwest Asia planting and harvesting more productive cereal grains and the domestication of cattle (aurochs), sheep and goats created the foundation of what we know today as an agricultural economy that lead to the formation of the first agrarian state.

Clearly agriculture has the advantage that a larger amount of food can be produced from the same area of land, supporting a population that has likely already outgrown the carrying capacity of the region through traditional hunting and gathering subsistence patterns. Some studies have suggested that the early ratio may be six or seven to one in terms of agricultural productivity over hunting and gathering per unit of land. It is also clear that it takes more labor to plant, cultivate, harvest, and process plant material. As mentioned earlier agriculture requires more work and results in less leisure time than hunting-gathering.

It is also less of a broad-spectrum subsistence strategy because it results in an overall reduction in the variety of plants and animals that can be exploited. This can lead to nutritional deficiencies and the associated diseases such as scurvy and rickets. Paleolithic and Epipaleolithic hunter-gatherers likely had better balanced diets than many early agriculturalists. Sedentary agriculturalists were also generally more vulnerable to famine due to local climatic variations than their mobile hunter-gatherer predecessors because they could not move their houses and fields into more favorable areas. They also would likely have been more vulnerable to gastrointestinal infections due to poor sanitary conditions and infectious epidemics due to crowded living (sometimes in very close association with livestock).

An increased reliance on cultivated complex carbohydrates in the diet also resulted in an increase in tooth wear due to sand particles produced by grinding seeds between a mano and metate (mortal and pestal) and an increase in tooth decay and cavities (caries) due to the sugars produced by carbohydrate consumption. There is much debate and discussion today among nutritionists and medical professionals about the effects of less daily exercise, more carbohydrates and simple sugars, and fewer fruits and vegetables (instead of grains) on the overall health of the modern population and the growing prevalence of diabetes and heart disease, all of which seem to be related to a sedentary lifestyle.

Agriculture limits mobility, requires more elaborate storage methods, and necessitates defending the stored food from outsiders, which requires a more complex social organization and hierarchy. We see examples of inter-village conflict in agricultural societies, an increase in elite paraphernalia, and the appearance of defensive structures that are not present in hunter-gatherer societies.

In archaeology the quest for food and the production of food are subsistence activities. Subsistence strategies will vary with the environment, local landforms, mobility patterns, and population levels. In the study of prehistoric societies without market trading or today's central banks, subsistence activities are considered *economic* activities.

One thing is clear. Once populations grow to a large enough level it is simply not economically feasible for large groups to revert to hunting and gathering because the carrying capacity of the land cannot support large human populations through hunting and gathering. We see occasional cases when sedentary agriculturists switch to hunting and gathering but these are usually associated with some environmental crisis or result from intergroup hostilities and warfare that forces a group to abandon their settlements.

Before leaving this section, it is important to remember that Paleolithic and Mesolithic (or Epipaleolithic) people harvested a wide variety of wild plant materials and could store them, at least for short periods of time, before moving on to other locations. When ripe fruits and wild grains are stored they can ferment. The natural fermentation process can produce alcoholic beverages. Several studies have suggested that the ultimate origins of agriculture, or at least selective plant domestication sometimes, may have had more to do with the production of alcoholic beverages, perhaps for ritual or ceremonial consumption, than for food consumption. This, like so many other topics in this book, is an ongoing area of investigation.

7 STATES AND CIVILIZATIONS AND THEIR RISE AND FALL

What is civilization? The answer may not be as clear as it seems.

A common checklist for a civilization requires the presence of a formal government (usually with hereditary leaders with absolute power), social stratification with an elite class (usually hereditary), large and dense settlements, agriculture, monumental edifices and public architecture, elaborate burials of (hereditary) elites (with exotic, rare, and highly crafted materials), large organized armies, full-time trade specialists (usually called artisans), and recordkeeping (usually in the form of writing). If you have all these then you can say you have a civilization. If one is lacking then you don't have a civilization, instead you have a complex chiefdom, according to many.

This is based to a large degree on Elman Service who created a four-part matrix that generally categorizes human societies as either hunter-gatherers, segmentary societies (early agriculturists), chiefdoms (agriculturalists with hereditary leaders), and states (with their associated complexity) (Service 1962, Wright 1978). I use this matrix in all of my classes. It is that important. You will see later that there may be exceptions to this rule (particularly in terms of the Mongol Empire).

Another approach to this whole issue is to accept a broader archaeological definition which is that a civilization is shorthand for urbanized states (an important distinction). Agrarian pre-industrial civilizations based on cities with large populations and complex social organizations (usually with hereditary elites and rulers) that rely on the centralized accumulation of capital (wealth) through tribute and taxation of the laboring and slave classes are then, by this definition civilizations (Cowgill, 2004, Fagan 2007:293). Note the inclusion of slaves here, more on that later.

So what is a "state"? According to most archaeologists we must refer to the Service checklist above except that early states have lower populations and smaller urban centers than later ones. The dividing lines can become blurred and so "civilization" is an emotionally loaded and ambiguous term, but does <u>not</u> imply that civilizations (or states) are morally or ethically or evolutionarily superior to other forms of social organization, they are merely different, and much more complex. In the greater scheme of things, you will see that civilizations are a recent invention.

An early city, by some definitions must generally have a population of at least about 5,000 people and must be larger than the neighboring towns or villages. It is a "central place" in the local geography and is more complex in its social organization. A population of 5.000 today barely qualifies as a tiny municipality, but remember we are not using today's standards.

V. Gordon Childe coined the term "Neolithic Revolution" (discussed earlier). He also coined the term "Urban Revolution" (1950:3). He considered technology and craft specialization as key to developing urban civilizations. He worked and wrote in the early to mid-20th century and his ideas were very sophisticated for the time yet seem somewhat simplistic today. Yet, his views seem to permeate our contemporary modern ideas about what civilization is and how it developed, which suggest some type of "sticky" power that defies the later evidence. Childe, as a person of his time, seemed to be somewhat preoccupied with social and political revolutions (such as those associated with World One and World War Two).

There are several semi-classic theories about the emergence of the state. One is that warfare is a key factor, one is that states grow, mature, age, and die like human organisms, and another is that they intensified their productivity through technology and increased central control. Yes, but yet another approach is a multivariate approach suggesting agriculture, warfare, religion, technology, social control, and local resources all play a varying role. Another suggests the state is a "living system" based on agriculture, technology and religion. Another is focused on the environment and leadership, based on what is available. There are also social theories about the emergence of the state that focus on social, economic, and political power, and the ability of a charismatic individual to assume the mantle of leadership, and then to maintain control by force.

As in the origins of agriculture, there is likely a multiplicity of causes, all are necessary and none are individually sufficient, for the origin of the state. It is almost as if it takes the "perfect storm" involving many factors for state formation to occur (Adams 1966, Carnerio 1970).

The world's first states were politically centralized and politically stratified societies. They developed in only a few locations such as Mesopotamia, Egypt, Mexico, the Andes, China, and a few other areas.

One popular theory about the origin of states is that they grew out of situations where a group of chiefdoms were competing with one another; eventually one competitor achieved dominance over its neighbors and merged the others into a larger political unit. This is a sort of "first to market" approach in modern economic terms, and once one leader achieves this status the "barriers to entry" for other potential usurpers become high, and it is literally life or death -- and usually death for the usurper (Carnerio 1970).

Once achieved, leaders of early states often legitimized their positions by acknowledging the various religious traditions of their subjects but managed eventually assumed the status of a god in one or more of the traditions. Remember, we are talking about a period when the leader was absolute and eager for legitimization. Early examples suggest this transmutation occurred after they died, in later examples we see living rulers assuming the mantle of "sacred legitimization" and god status while they were living

When the ruler of a state dies another must rise to take his place. If there is no succession tradition in place this can often lead to civil unrest. We see this repeatedly. Some states and empires (a group of states ruled or administered centrally) simply vanish from the record (into the dust) when there is no one to fill the power vacuum left behind by the death of the "supreme leader".

There is a theory that the early civilizations declined due to the economic rule of diminishing marginal returns, this also relates to why hunter-gatherers move around (Keene 1981). Once complexity reached a certain level, and the elite class became too large due to hereditary titles and perks, and agricultural production declined due to salination and soil depletion or other reasons, and local resources diminished, while the population grows and reaches its peak, then to top it off something like a draught occurs, decline was inevitable (for more on decline and disorganization see Crumley 1995, Frahm 2013, Hole 1994,, McGuire 2996, Smith 2003,

Tainter 1988, Smith 2000, Webster 2002, Yoffee 1993). Remember, archaeology is about the rise <u>and fall,</u> of societies large and small.

Keep in mind that most civilizations do not die as biological organisms do. They are not born, act as infants, grow to adulthood, mature, get old, and inevitably die in 40 to 70 years, which is a concept in the popular mind that predates Darwin (Gibbon 1804). They result from social circumstances that require them to invent and reinvent themselves often over, and over, and when they cannot do that, or outside circumstances intervene, then they die or transform into something else. Most agrarian preindustrial civilizations have gone through cycles of formative development, growth, fluorescence, and then decline many times (so have many modern corporations). Some reinvent themselves for a while, then they disappear, some (or their traditions) remain with us today. Sometimes these cycles last for hundreds of years, sometimes for thousands. Sometimes they last just decades. The blink of an archaeological eye.

Most original states (and civilizations) were to one degree or another based on sedentary agriculture. Discussed earlier. There are theories that that relate to the ecological potential of river floodplains and to irrigation agriculture. Both are concerned with hydrological civilizations. There are theories about technology and trade, and about exchange systems (bartering, reciprocity, redistribution, and market based economies). The theories about the origin of the state and the appearance of civilizations are as varied as the theories about agriculture, but many think that a central control over religion and violence (belief systems, warfare and armed civil control) are critical (necessary but not necessarily sufficient).

Let us pause here and repeat that being in a civilization does not mean you are civilized. Civil behavior, by our modern definition, has nothing to do with the definition of civilization. Despots, warlords, tyrants, totalitarians, and self-serving megalomaniacs can rule urban states and even empires. This is more the rule than the exception (they are successful partly based on traits that would get them ostracized in a hunter-gatherer setting).. By our modern standards nothing is civilized about them or their behavior, but they do have at least temporary control over their political/economic domain. All great men, it seems, are not necessarily good men (or women)..

Having both slaves and leaders based on their parenthood and inherited wealth instead of their abilities, with the lower classes living in densely packed quarters may not sound very "civilized" to the modern ear. So clearly, civilizations do not necessarily need to embrace modern Western concepts liberty, freedom, justice, democracy, science, and technology. These values are more about how we define ourselves today.

I have said several times that archaeology is the study of the rise and fall of societies large and small. I heard Brian Fagan say this at a lecture and I never forgot it. Remember that none of the archaic or agrarian states I will describe in these pages are with us any more (with the possible exception of China). That is the one thing they all have in common. They are all, or mostly all, gone.

Rising complexity is a key characteristic of early states, and of the modern world. Is it inevitable? Is it sustainable? It seems characterized by an ever-intensifying spiral of many things all of human origin: economic, technological, religious, social and political. As long as we do not exceed the carrying capacity of our "system" (which today is the planet), if we somehow "ratchet up" our food production (largely through technology and agricultural intensification techniques) and as long as people continue to believe in the process, then things continue to work.

In the archaeological realm none have proven sustainable in their original form, they all died or transformed. I am reminded of a line from the popular movie *Jurassic Park* where Jeff Goldblum says, "Life will find a way" (Kennedy and Moderm, 1993). Although it is biological in intent, it has strong cultural implications.

In the realm of international relations, I am also reminded of a quote attributed to Henry Kissinger, "There is not now, nor has there ever been, a true international community with shared values; humanity forever lives on the edge of conflict. Thus, only realistic statecraft, aimed at balancing competing national interests, can succeed." (Kissinger 2014). In a short summary the best we can realistically hope for is a short truce. This attributed quote presumes an understanding of what a "nation" is, (which is lightly touched on below) and a deep understanding of the concept of culture.

It is worth nothing that the modern concept of "nation" seems to date to the mid 1600's with the end of the 30 years' war in Europe and the Westphalian Treaties (about the same time that Ussher wrote about the age of humanity). At that time, it seems that many Western political jurisdictions were unintentionally yet permanently separated from the religious/political rulers of antiquity, at least marginally (Armstrong 2014).

The origin of the Western notion of the <u>separation</u> of the state and religion … and rulers who claimed legitimacy from "above" (not from the people) dates generally to this time.

Note that Kissinger's view of diplomacy (based on the quote above) belies a sophisticated understanding of the application of the term culture, which includes "shared values", and resonates in my mind as a prime example of why archaeology (and anthropology) matter today because we teach our students about this and it does not need to be applied only to prehistory or non-urbanized societies.

Table 2. Southwest Asia and Mesopotamia
Unless otherwise stated dates are the beginning or earliest dates

Approx. Lakh Time	Key Event, Time Period, or Site	Approx. Date
11:59 PM	Today	
11:58 PM	Sputnik 1 Launched, Space Age Begins	1957
11:16 PM	Cyrus the Great Annexes Babylon	539 BCE
11:02 PM	Assyrians Appear	1,400 BCE
10:52 PM	Mesopotamian Delta Irrigated, Babylonians	2,000 BCE
10:47 PM	Akkadian Empire and Sargon	2,334 BCE
10:47 PM	City of Ur	2,300 BCE
10:35 PM	Sumerians and Nascent World System	3,000 BCE
10:27 PM	City of Uruk	3,500 BCE
10:22 PM	Conflict (Tell Brak)	3,800 BCE
10:02 PM	Gulf of Oman reaches current level	5,000 BCE
9:46 PM	Catalhoyuk abandoned (Turkey)	6,000 BCE
9:37 PM	Ubiad Chiefdoms in Delta Lowlands	6,500 BCE
9:37 PM	Halafian Painted Wares, Chiefdoms	6,500 BCE
9:29 PM	Schmandt-Besserat (tokens)	7,000 BCE
9:21 PM	Catalhoyuk begins (Turkey)	7,500 BCE
9:12 PM	Use of Small Clay Tokens for Trade	8,000 BCE
9:12 PM	Regional Trade in Obsidian and Other Materials	8,000 BCE
9:11 PM	Herding and Farming Zargos Mtns, PPNB	8,500 BCE
9:04 PM	Small villages and farming, PPNA	8,500 BCE
8:59 PM	Cultivation of Wild Plants in Fertile Crescent	8,800 BCE
8:44 PM	Younger Dryas (cold snap) Ends	9,650 BCE
8:44 PM	Gobekli Tepe	9,700 BCE
8:39 PM	Site of Jericho,, Late Natufian (Neolithic)	10,000 BCE
8:23 PM	Younger Dryas (cold snap) Begins	10,950 BCE
8:22 PM	Holocene Begins	11,000 BCE
7:55 PM	Early Natufian	12,600 BCE

8 SOUTHWEST ASIA AND MESOPOTAMIA

Regional Overview

Mesopotamia means "the land between two rivers" and it is the cradle of what we know as civilization (discussed above). The area between the Tigris and Euphrates rivers in modern day Iran is home the first agrarian states we see anywhere in the world. The Tigris River is to the north (it flows through the present-day city of Bagdad) and the Euphrates River is to the south, and at their closest points they are less than 50 miles apart. Both are easily navigable. A larger region that encompasses Mesopotamia extends from the Persian Gulf of all the way west to the Mediterranean, forming a crescent shape, and is referred to as the "Fertile Crescent".

At the height of the last glacial maximum, about 15,000 BCE, both the Tigris and Euphrates flowed into the Persian Gulf about 500 miles further south than today. The area experienced flooding for several thousand years as the glaciers melted. Not surprisingly, one of the oldest written stories in the world, *The Epic of* Gilgamesh (Mitchell 2004), is from this region and contains a narrative about a flood event very similar to the story of Noah's Ark in the Old Testament. By about 5000 BCE the shoreline reached modern limits and actually rose several feet above current levels. This is a period called the "climatic optimum".

The Neolithic

The region known as Southwest Asia was cool and dry immediately after the last Ice Age at about 10,000 BCE. Human populations were sparse and highly mobile as forests gradually spread throughout the region. This climatic change favored wild annual cereal grasses such as wheat, barley, and rye. Early farmers hunted gazelles, wild cattle (aurochs), sheep, goats and other species. Possibly within a generation or two by about 9000 BCE it appears that some of the population switched to herding sheep and goats and growing emmer wheat, barley, lentils, and peas. The causes for this transition are key to understanding the possible origins of agriculture and domestication.

The early Neolithic site of Gobekli Tepe, in southeast Turkey, dates to approximately 9700 BCE It consists of pairs of T-shaped limestone monoliths carved with images of human arms and hands and also of wild animals. There is little evidence of domestic occupation and it seems that this was a "central place" for ceremonial group activities by the hunter-gatherer population(s) of the region. It may have been utilized over a period of nearly 1,500 years. It is important for many reasons, but one is that it seems to demonstrate that hunter-gatherers created monumental architecture and ceremonial places (which some say is a defining characteristic of a state).

By about 8000 BCE there is evidence of herding and farming in the highlands (near the Zargos Mountains) and the establishment of small villages. Many settlements became trading centers and by about 8000 BCE the numbers of imported materials and exotic objects rose dramatically. Trade goods included obsidian from Anatolia, turquoise from Sinai, and seashells from the Mediterranean and Red Sea. Many of these trade items were apparently kept track of using small clay tokens which may have been precursors of the earliest form of writing (for accounting purposes) (Schmandt-Besserat 1992).

By about 7000 BCE highland people had settled in northern Mesopotamia and took advantage of rainfall agriculture. There was considerable variation in farming cultures throughout the region, probably due to local cultural trajectories. There is little evidence of social hierarchy or elites. Most likely the early agricultural societies operated through kinship lineages.

By about 6500 BCE the Halafian culture appeared over a wide area of northern Mesopotamia (in what is today northern Iraq) and in Anatolia (Turkey). It is characterized by painted pottery and is also believed to be home to the first chiefdoms in the region. The first lowland farming communities date to about 5,800 BCE and are known as the Ubaid culture. They generally covered about 10 hectares (a hectare is about the size of two American football fields) and housed 2,000 to 4,000 people at a given time. It is generally believed that the Ubaid culture was the precursor to later Mesopotamian civilization. Mass burials such as one at Tell Barak, in northeast Syria, date to about 3800 BCE and provide evidence of violent conflict between or within the farming communities (Watkins 2013).

Of note is that by 2000 BCE the Mesopotamian Delta had been completely modified by human activity, including irrigation that lead to a rise in the salt content of the soil and a drastic drop in crop yields. The early human agricultural activity combined with a warming regional climate and lowering water tables made agriculture more difficult and the resulting arid landscape persists today (Wilkinson 2003).

Anatolia and Catalhoyuk

Anatolia is modern day Turkey. It lies on the northwest extreme of the region we define as southwest Asia. It plays a very important part in the development of both southwest Asia and the Mediterranean.

The village of Catalhoyuk in southeast Anatolia dates to approximately 7500 BCE. It was occupied for over a thousand years and was abandoned in approximately 6000 BCE. What is interesting to archaeologists about this large village is that it has been extensively studied for decades and has shed a great deal of light on this period of our prehistory (Hodder 2006).

The village was originally settled in a marshy area where the inhabitants hunted local game and harvested wild grains and plants. Later there is evidence of plant and animal domestication at this site. It provides us with evidence of earliest subsistence strategies in the region. Also, it lies on the fringe of the northeastern Natufian culture range, in what is known as the Pre-Pottery Neolithic period (probably hundreds of books have been written on this period, it is so important).

Catalhoyuk is located near an obsidian source and the inhabitants were engaged in widespread trading throughout the region. It is a large tell (mound) that was built up through successive layers of construction and occupies approximately 13 hectares (about 26 football fields). Its layout is considered a classic example of a segmentary society where kinship and family lineages form the foundation for a social structure that exists without a formal leader. The village had no public spaces, or even streets.

The architecture consists of family domiciles accessed through the roof. Successive layers of construction repeat the layout of the earlier domiciles located directly below. There is evidence that the occupants would occasionally dig into earlier layers, perhaps to retrieve something of special value, and this suggests family lineage continuity in the same location that may have spanned a thousand years or more (assuming 5 generations per century this means 50 generations of one lineage may have lived in the same location). Some of the domestic units were rebuilt, one on top of another, at least a dozen times.

There is little evidence of social stratification at this site and burials suggest a certain equality between the sexes. Ancestors were often buried below the floors of the living areas. Sometimes, skulls of certain individuals were carefully plastered to recreate their facial characteristics, complete with seashell eyes, and then buried with other individuals. This suggests a form of ancestor worship and/or kinship affinity. It is also similar to the plaster skulls in nearby Jericho which suggests cultural connections.

Catalhoyuk is famous for the plaster murals depicting hunters in what appear to be leopard skin loincloths that appear to chase wild cattle (aurochs) and boar. Millennia later, in Anatolia, we have reference to the significance of leopard skin cloaks through Homer's Iliad where Paris leaves the safety of Troy to fight the invading Greeks wearing a leopard skin cloak. I find this to be intriguing and another piece of evidence that suggests a long line of cultural continuity in the region.

Figurines and bas relief sculptures, and plastered bulls' heads (complete with horns) in the domiciles suggest a complex social and ritual life. Reverence for the fertility of females is suggested in the famous "mother goddess" clay sculpture depicting a voluptuous seated female giving birth while flanked by two leopards.

Archaeologist Ian Hodder has studied Catalhoyuk for decades and suggests that because it spans the entire spectrum of plant and animal domestication, is focused on the habitus, or home, and the associated domestic activities associated with the "domus" that it may provide evidence that before humans could domesticate plants and animals we first had to domesticate ourselves, and that early effort failed (Balter, 2005, Hodder and Cessford 2004).

Catalhoyuk was ultimately abandoned about 6000 BCE and the occupants converted to life in smaller villages scattered over the landscape. Although never a true city in the classic sense, it was a large community that is an icon for the transition from hunting and gathering to a sedentary agricultural lifestyle, to the importance of the family and kinship, and to the potential for long-term continuity in human social endeavors (if only for a couple thousand years). It also apparently failed to develop the necessary administrative and social mechanisms to cope with the increased complexity of the settlement and its trading networks and was ultimately abandoned. As such, it represents an early, but unsuccessful, experiment in urbanization.

Uruk – One of the World's First Cities

The city of Uruk was located in Mesopotamia near the Euphrates River in modern-day Iraq and dates to perhaps just before 3500 BCE, before the earliest Sumerian states, and about 2000 years after Catalhoyuk. It is important because it is one of the oldest true cities in the world and is described in The *Epic of Gilgamesh* (Mitchell 2004) in amazing detail "See how its ramparts gleam like copper in the sun. Climb the stone staircase, more ancient than the mind can imagine …" During its fluorescence Uruk may also have been the largest city in the world at the time, like a modern New York. It is pronounced two ways; "Uruk" or "Iraq". It occupied an area of about 80 hectares (about 160 football fields), was enclosed by a wall, and contained the Ziggurat of Inanna. By 3500 BCE – less than sixty years after Uruk) other true cities had come into being in almost every corner of the Iranian Plateau and on the borders of Afghanistan.

The Sumerians

By about 3000 BCE we see the appearance of the earliest civilization in the world, the Sumerians (see the earlier discussion above for the archaeological definition of "civilization"). The Sumerian elites used a lavish display of prestige items and exotic luxuries to anchor their social prestige and authority. The Sumerians were the center of something called a "nascent world system", which was linked through trade with the Indus Valley to the east and the Mediterranean and Nile Valley to the west. Cylinder seals provide a good example. They were used to seal pegs and coverings to containers to exert administrative control (just like your luggage might be sealed with an embossed plastic tie by the TSA after being inspected today). The cylindrical seals were rolled over wet clay and embossed images of conquest and control, of kings and captives. Some seals depict scenes from *The Epic of Gilgamesh*. These seals have been found as far away as the Indus Valley and provide evidence of administrative control and a vast trade network. It also suggests a "grounding" in ideology based on past events (Algaze 2001).

Older than the pyramids of Egypt, Sumerian and pre-Sumerian ziggurats were staged towers surrounded by shrines and accessed by staircases. They would have required the control over a large labor force to construct and were built to a traditional design concept. They were several stories high and would have been a visible symbol of political and religious control over the relatively flat landscape of Lower Mesopotamia.

The Sumerian city of Ur dates to about 2300 BCE and the residential and specialty crafts areas were dwarfed by a large ziggurat. The Royal Cemetery was excavated in 1927-28 by Sir Leonard Wooley; the royal burial of Queen Pu-abi for example included dozens of sacrificed retainers including musicians, grooms, soldiers, oxen, and carts. The appearance of ritual human sacrifice in this example is characteristic of many elite burials in early civilizations throughout the world.

While the Sumerian civilization was probably the earliest civilization in the world, it never became an empire. The region was never politically unified under one ruler. Instead the elites and the soldiers of the city-states vied for supremacy and rose to fluorescence and fell into oblivion relatively frequently, perhaps every few generations (Matthews, 2013). The Sumerians also appear to have developed maritime trade through the Persian Gulf.

The Appearance of Writing

According to the Schmandt-Besserat sequence the earliest writing developed in this region as a method of record keeping associated with trade. Writing appears to have its origins as a method of accounting. By 7000 BCE clay tokens in just over a dozen shapes (such as cones, spheres, and disks) were apparently used to represent a quantity of grain being traded and/or transported. By 4,000 (three thousand years later) there were over 300 shapes.

By 3500 BCE (just 500 years later) the clay tokens were generally stored together in circular sealed clay "envelopes" with impressions of the tokens on the outside of the "envelope". By 3200 BCE (just 300 years later) the clay tokens had disappeared and were replaced by their impressions on the envelopes. By 3100 BCE (just a few generations later) the envelopes disappeared and the images of the tokens were impressed on clay tablets. It is generally believed this was the precursor to later cuneiform text (the world's first writing) (Robinson 2007, Schmandt-Besserat 1992, 1981).

The earliest cuneiform pictographs date to about 3000 BCE. The pictographic images eventually became more abstract and cuneiform stylus "writing" dates to about 2400 BCE then was a stylistically modified at about 700 BCE. Literate specialists such as scribes would have held prestigious positions within the palaces and communities. We know from excavations at places like Elba in northern Syria that by about 2400 BCE the clay tablets with cuneiform stylus impressions were stored on wooden shelves, much like books are stored in a library today. The texts are generally focused on administrative and economic records although we also see the earliest literary pieces in cuneiform during this period, such as *The Epic of Gilgamesh*.

The Akkadians and the World's First Empire

At about 3000 BCE a new state had emerged in central Mesopotamia (north of the Sumerians) in a strategic geographic position at the center of a network of regional trade routes. It was the Elamite state. These trade routes joined widely separated communities on the Iranian Plateau through a complex interaction sphere. Major trading centers within the state developed near sources of lapis lazuli, turquoise, chlorite, and other materials.

By about 2800 BCE several city-states were scattered over all of Mesopotamia, each headed by a ruler who vied with neighboring city-states for power, status, and prestige. Trade had also expanded north into Anatolia. By 2500 BCE Akkadian cities in the formerly Elamite region north of Syria were competing with lowland cities for trade and power. In 2334 BCE a Semitic-speaking Akkadian named Sargon founded a ruling dynasty in a town named Agade south of Babylon. He also founded the town of Akkad, which has never been located. Known as Sargon, he engaged in commercial ventures and military campaigns and created the first empire in the region that included both Sumer and northern Mesopotamia. This was the Akkadian Empire which lasted from 2334-2,79 BCE (a mere 55 years). Succession issues apparently doomed this empire to a short duration, as you will see happened to many others.

Later, Babylon's greatness culminated in the reign of Hammurabi in 1792 BCE. Hammurabi integrated the smaller kingdoms of Mesopotamia for a short period, but like Akkad, his empire declined soon after his death. Hammurabi is perhaps best known for the Hammurabi Code which is considered by many to be the first written law. It basically protected the rights of the rich and powerful and provided punishments for commoners and slaves, but it was an important codification of "law" that protected people from the "whims" of a total dictator and promised a certain degree of predictability in terms of crime and punishment.

The Assyrians

In the late second millennium BCE, the city of Assur in the northern part of Mesopotamia rose to power. The Assyrian empire was noted for its "grandiloquent and despotic rulers who engaged in annual campaigns of military conquest and who boasted of their conquests on their palace walls" (Fagan and Duranni 2014:324). During the first millennium BCE, the Assyrian Empire stretched from the Mediterranean all the way to the Persian Gulf and controlled the entire Fertile Crescent. The Assyrian Empire fell in 612 BCE and left a power vacuum briefly filled by the neighboring Babylonians under Nebuchadnezzar. The Babylonian empire later fell to Cyrus the Great and the Persian Empire in 539 BCE (a very important time in history but this book is largely about prehistory).

This may sound like a boring lineage of states and empires that rose and fell but remember the very small geographic area associated with their "world" at the time and how interconnected they all were. Also remember how briefly these important first experiments in governance and social organization lasted. It suggests how fragile our social, economic, and political institutions really are, even today (more on this in the last chapter).

THE LONG WALK HERE

Table 3. The Mediterranean
Unless otherwise stated dates are the beginning or earliest dates

Approx. Lakh Time	Key Event, Time Period, or Site	Approx. Date
11:59 PM	Today	
11:58 PM	Sputnik 1 Launched, Space Age Begins	1957
11:32 PM	Roman Empire Splits in Two	395
11:32 PM	Visigoths from Europe Sack Rome	410
11:31 PM	Constantine – Christianity	313
11:25 PM	Gregorian Calendar Start Date	1
11:24 PM	Julius Caesar Conquers Gaul	51 BCE
11:23 PM	Rome Destroys Carthage	146 BCE
11:20 PM	Alexander the Great Dies	323 BCE
11:13 PM	Etruscans Fortify Rome	753 BCE
11:09 PM	Athens Fluorescence	1,000 BCE
11:09 PM	Phoenicians	1,000 BCE
11:09 PM	Villanovans Arrive from Europe	1,000 BCE
11:04 PM	Kadesh Peace Treaty (Hittite and Egypt)	1,286 BCE
11:03 PM	Uluburun Shipwreck	1,320 BCE
11:02 PM	Mycenaeans	1,400 BCE
10:58 PM	Hittites	1,650 BCE
10:57 PM	Thera Eruption (Minoan Demise)	1,700 BCE
10:52 PM	Minoan First Palace Period - Maritime	2,000 BCE
10:47 PM	Troy II	2,300 BCE
10:35 PM	Cycladic Peoples	3,200 BCE
10:35 PM	Troy I	3,000 BCE
10:19 PM	Fortified Villages in Anatolia	4,000 BCE
8:44 PM	Younger Dryas (cold snap) Ends	9,650 BCE
8:23 PM	Younger Dryas (cold snap) Begins	10,950 BCE
8:22 PM	Holocene Begins	11,000 BCE
7:15 PM	Glacial Maximum	15,000 BCE

9 THE MEDITERRANEAN

This is a complex region that also is briefly covered in the chapters on Europe and Southwest Asia.

Regional Overview

The Mediterranean, particularly the Eastern Mediterranean region, includes what we today call Greece and Mycenae, Crete, Anatolia (Turkey), and the western portions of the Middle East (particularly Lebanon, Israel, Palestine, western Syria, and northern Egypt). The prehistory of the region is a complex mosaic of trade and migration over long distances both on land and by sea (sea craft and transport is an under-studied area in archaeology). By the time of the Romans the entire region could be considered a "civilized lake" that is seen by many as an expanded nascent regional economic system (which at the time was the extent of the known world). Remember, we first saw concept of a "nascent world system" with the Sumerians in Mesopotamia.

Wild goats, sheep, cattle (aurochs), barley, wheat, fermentable grapes, and olives with fish and rich maritime resources provided the basics for subsistence in a relatively temperate coastal, island, and inland environment. In a way this chapter is a sub-chapter of the earlier discussions about the Neanderthals in Europe, the later migration of *Homo sapiens* into Europe, and developing agriculture and sedentary village life in Southwest Asia. Although, by this time the Neanderthals were long gone and the region was becoming a virtual hotbed of trade and the exchange of ideas, technology, culture and ... genes. For more on this region see Alcock and Cherry 2013.

Cyclades and Troy

By about 4000 BCE small fortified villages flourished in Anatolia, one, Troy I, dates to about 3000 BCE, Troy II dates to about 2300 BCE and contained elaborate architecture and finely work gold and bronze items. Although an inland city, Troy was only about 2.5 miles from a well-protected bay at the mouth of the Dardanelles River which provided a strategic nautical advantage. It plays an important role later in time, much like Babylon did regionally in the past. Local chiefdoms were widely scattered throughout the region. By this time agriculture had been established for thousands of years and Anatolians were trading widely over the region and into the Aegean Sea where the Cycladic peoples to the west were thriving (from about 3200 BCE to about 2000 BCE). Today the Cycladic people are best known for their "modernistic" white marble sculptures, which are widely sought in museums and private collections.

Minoans

By about 2000 BCE the Minoan civilization apparently developed on the island of Crete. It lasted until approximately 1450 BCE. The demise of the Minoans left a power vacuum of sorts in the region later filled partly by the Phoenicians to the south and partly by the Mycenaeans to the northwest. The Minoans were largely agricultural villagers and a seafaring people. The ruling elite occupied large palaces that were typically arranged around a central court with workshops, residential areas, bathing areas, and kitchen areas surrounding the huge central courtyard. The Minoan palaces, such as the palace at Knossos, were not fortified (although the island itself could be seen as a fortress). Knossos is considered by some to be Europe's first city.

The collapse of the Minoan civilization may be partly attributed to a huge volcanic eruption on the island of Thera (otherwise known as Santorini) in the seventeenth century BCE. This eruption, to the north of Crete, may have produced a tsunami that wreaked havoc on the powerful Minoan fleets and decimated the northern coastline. Some consider the much later Greek legend of the lost continent of Atlantis to be associated with this event. Extensive Minoan maritime trade networks extended from Sardinia in the west to Anatolia, to the Levant, and to Egypt. An undeciphered script, Linear A, is associated with Minoan palace and religious writings.

Evidence of this trade network is contained in the wrecks of seagoing ships of the time, such as the famous late 14th century BCE Uluburun shipwreck (discovered in 1982 under 150 feet of water) just off the southern coast of Anatolia. The shipwreck is tentatively dated at about 1320 BCE.

A review of the ship's cargo includes 350 copper ingots from Cyprus, a ton of tin ingots (both of which would have been used to make bronze weapons, tools, and other objects), 100 ingots of cobalt-blue and turquoise glass, a ton of special resin (for cosmetics or perfume), ebony logs from Egypt, elephant tusks, hippopotamus teeth, ostrich and tortoise shells, and fruits and spices. Other items include a gold scarab of Queen Nefertiti. The ship apparently was traveling clockwise around the eastern Mediterranean (following the prevailing winds) before it sank, presumably in a storm.

Hittites

The Hittites rose to dominance in Anatolia in about 1650 BCE (while the Minoans were flourishing to the west). Their power was based largely on diplomatic and trading networks until about 1200 BCE when trade networks in the eastern Mediterranean collapsed, possibly due to the work of a little-known group generally called the "Sea People" who we may today just call "pirates". Again, the importance of maritime activity in the eastern Mediterranean cannot be over-estimated. The Hittites were a parliamentary monarchy (perhaps the first) and are known today for the Kadesh peace treaty with Ramses II and Egypt which dates to 1286 BCE. This is one of the earliest "international" peace treaties and is inscribed on the walls of the United Nations building façade in New York.

Phoenicians

By the first millennium BCE the Phoenicians had largely re-established trade through the region and had founded cities in the Levant such as Tyre, Sidon, and Byblos. The Phoenicians were almost everywhere in the Mediterranean by 800 BCE and their fleets traded in both raw materials and manufactured goods. They developed their own script by about 700 BCE and there is evidence this script may have influenced later Greek writing. The city of Carthage was originally a Phoenician colony and later the center of an empire that dominated the Mediterranean in the first millennium BCE before being destroyed by the Romans in 146 BCE.

Greece and Mycenae

Shortly after the demise of the Minoan civilization the Mycenaeans rose to dominance in what is today Greece and Mycenae. This occurred about

1400 BCE and lasted until about 1150 BCE (about 250 years). There is evidence of Minoan and Hittite influence in Mycenaean architecture. Like the Minoans, the Mycenaeans were largely villagers. Mycenaean palaces, like the famous site of Mycenae, were fortified with controlled access and a central throne room that bears architectural resemblance to Minoan palaces (with fortified walls).

Heinrich Schliemann conducted excavations at both Mycenae and Troy in the early twentieth century. Although his dating was off and his methods were crude one of his discoveries was a gold burial mask he incorrectly proclaimed to be the legendary Agamemnon, the leader of the conquest of Troy. The Mycenaeans were a military society with a well-organized army and their own writing system, which is linked to the undeciphered Minoan Linear A script.

Under the influence of Mycenae small city-states flourished throughout what is today Greece and Macedonia. These city-states were autonomous and they came together generally only in the face of a common threat, (such as the Persian invaders from Anatolia in the fifth century BCE). Later, during the period of "classical" Greek civilization the democratic city-state of Athens, with its famous marketplace, democracy, and Parthenon, rose to dominance.

In the late fourth century Alexander the Great, the aristocratic son of Phillip II of Macedonia, raised an army and launched an invasion of Anatolia that would eventually include Greece, all of the eastern Mediterranean, Egypt, former Babylonia, and parts of India. Alexander the Great's empire fragmented after his death in 323 BCE, largely due to succession issues. It is worth noting that his initial victories against the Persian Empire (remember Cyrus the Great) formed the geographic foundation for his new empire. I have always been fascinated by the fact that Socrates taught Plato, Plato taught Aristotle, and apparently Aristotle (a Greek) taught Alexander (a Macedonian).

Etruscans and Rome

By approximately 1000 BCE a group of migrants from central Europe, known as the Urnfield people, had settled south of the Alps in the Po Valley. They developed bronze products traded throughout Italy and into central Europe. Knows as the Villanovan culture, they eventually produced iron tools and established a trading network over most of Italy. Eventually they became known as the Etruscans and they were the first to fortify the Seven Hills of Rome.

In 509 BCE the Etruscans were evicted by native Romans. The next few centuries saw the emergence of the city-state of Rome and the rise of the Imperial Roman Empire, which was based largely on the ruins of the western portion of the empire of Alexander the Great. It eventually extended all the way north to the Rhine and to the southern border of Scotland (which was unsuccessfully defended by something called "Hadrian's Wall"). In 51 BCE Julius Caesar finished his conquest Gaul (Northern Europe and England). This was just a few years after Rome destroyed Carthage (see above). In AD 313 the Roman emperor Constantine converted to Christianity.

In AD 395 the Roman Empire split into the eastern and western sections. The western section, after a series of complex interactions with Europe and elsewhere, would eventually produce what is commonly called today "Western Civilization" and the eastern portion pursued its own course with subsequent influence from Islam. In AD 410 the central Europeans (remember the Etruscans mentioned above) returned to Rome, as the Visigoths, who sacked and burned the city, which is an interesting turn of events to me given that migrant northern Europeans were involved in the founding of Rome.

Table 4. Europe
Unless otherwise stated dates are the beginning or earliest dates

Approx. Lakh Time	Key Event, Time Period, or Site	Approx. Date
11:59 PM	Today	
11:58 PM	Sputnik 1 Launched, Space Age Begins	1957
11:24 PM	Julius Caesar Conquers Gaul	51 BCE
11:17 PM	LA Tene Fortified Villages in Europe	500 BCE
11:12 PM	Halstatt Trade Networks	800 BCE
11:09 PM	Sythian Ironworking & Woven Rugs	1,000 BCE
10:52 PM	Urnfield Bronze	2,000 BCE
10:44 PM	Amesbury Archer	2,470 BCE
10:40 PM	Bell Beaker Society and Trade	2,700 BCE
10:35 PM	Wheeled Vehicles	3,000 BCE
10:35 PM	Ceremonial Landscapes with Megaliths	3,000 BCE
10:29 PM	Copper and Otzi the Iceman	3,350 BCE
10:25 PM	Plow Agriculture in Europe	3,600 BCE
10:19 PM	Agriculture in British Isles	4,000 BCE
10:10 PM	Megaliths Appear in France	4,500 BCE
10:02 PM	Bandkeramik Neolithic	5,000 BCE
9:45 PM	Neolithic in SE Europe and Coast	6,000 BCE
9:37 PM	Britain Becomes an Island	6,500 BCE
9:12 PM	Ireland Becomes an Island	8,000 BCE
8:44 PM	Younger Dryas (cold snap) Ends	9,650 BCE
8:23 PM	Younger Dryas (cold snap) Begins	10,950 BCE
8:22 PM	Holocene Begins	11,000 BCE
7:15 PM	Glacial Maximum	15,000 BCE

10 EUROPE

Regional Overview

Most people of European descent think of Europe as a continent. Many geographers take a different perspective and often view it as a peninsula jutting off of western Asia. Whichever perspective you take Europe is truly a "land between the oceans" (Cunliffe 2008).

The region is rich in natural resources and there are many ways to move around the peninsula, either by following river valleys (such as the Danube, truly the regional "superhighway" of prehistory) and mountain passes or by navigating the coastlines. It is estimated that the coastline of Europe (which also includes the Aegean) is approximately 23,000 miles long, equivalent to the circumference of the globe. Again (as said earlier), the archaeology of seafaring, if only by coastal navigation, has a long way to go.

Europe is named after Europa, the daughter of a Phoenician king (the Phoenician seafarers, were discussed earlier). According to Greek myth Europa captivated the attention of Zeus and eventually gave birth to their son Minos (of Crete).

At the end of the last Ice Age when sea levels were much lower, it was possible to walk from present day France to Britain (over a land expanse known as Doggerland). By 8000 BCE Ireland had been separated from the mainland and by 6500 BCE Britain had also become an island. Northern Europe also benefits from the powerful and warm and nutrient-rich North Atlantic Current. Some of the most productive fishing grounds include the seas around Ireland and the North Sea. The warmth of this current is so strong that it allows palm-like trees (known as "Cornish Palms") to grow in southern England.

As the ice retreated the vegetation and animal populations changed. Mammoth and wooly rhinoceros became extinct, reindeer and elk moved northwards. With the appearance of broad-leaved forests such as elm, oak, and hazel, smaller herbivores such as deer and cattle (aurochs) rose in population. This does not mean the area was uniform; localized environments were rich in many plant and animal resources. Because of the abundance of forest resources, early post-glacial hunter-gatherers moved around less than their Paleolithic ancestors and occupied their territory in smaller and more widely dispersed groups, perhaps centered on river valleys and coastal areas where marine resources were abundant, this is sometimes called broad-spectrum subsistence (Scarre 2013c).

Neolithic

Whether farming developed in Europe independently or was introduced from southwestern Asia is unknown. There is evidence supporting both concepts. By about 6000 BCE farming was well established in parts of the Aegean and southeastern Europe. It is thought by some that there may have been a "drift" of domestic animals and cereals from southwest Asia that were incorporated into existing European settlements.

Eastern and central Europe entered the Neolithic by approximately 5000 BCE with farming. This lead to more sedentary villages and a change from the broad-spectrum mobile hunting and gathering that typified the region for the previous several thousand years (during the Mesolithic or Epipaleolithic). The earliest farmers settled on the floodplains of rivers and streams, and near springs where the soil was naturally moist with natural pastureland. These farming communities appear to have occupied the same locations for centuries, just as the Anatolian and southwest Asian farmers had done.

Cardinal Ware Culture and Western European Peoples

By about 6000 BCE there were coastal agricultural communities in what is today Spain, southern France, and Italy. They have been identified by the distinctive cardium (cockle) shell impressions which first appear around 5600 BCE. This suggests there was a spread of pottery and domesticates into the region from other parts of the Mediterranean along the coastlines. For example, by about 5,000 BCE obsidian from southeast Asia appears on various islands, including Sardinia west of Italy (I did not mention it before but obsidian can be sourced based on its chemical components, all obsidian-producing volcanoes have different chemical signatures). By 4000 BCE internal fishing villages were thriving on the shores of Swiss Lakes.

Bankeramik (Danubian) Culture

The Bankeramik Culture occupied the middle Danube Valley by about 5000 BCE. They cultivated barley, einkorn, emmer wheat, and other crops. The Danube River connects Germany with the eastern Black Sea north of modern Turkey and it is thought by some that the Danube may have served as the "superhighway" of the time (mentioned earlier) connecting central Europe with southwestern Asia. The distribution of Bankeramik pottery throughout eastern Europe suggests this Danuban Culture was widespread.

The Bankeramik people lived in timber longhouses of fairly standardized construction and raised sheep and cattle. The early Bankeramik societies were apparently organized around social relationships that linked communities and tied people to the lands of their ancestors. Later, their burials suggest two important distinctions based on burial goods. The first is between males and females, and the second is between the young and the old.

Political power and social authority was apparently in the hands of older males who may have controlled cattle ownership and exchanges with other settlements. One example is the Varna cemetery. On the edge of the Black Sea, the Varna cemetery has produced richly furnished burials featuring copper, gold, and other ornaments that demonstrate the appearance of an elite class of powerful individuals by the 5th millennium BCE.

Another Bankeramik site is in southwest Germany provides evidence of conflict between villages. The Talheim "death pit" contains the jumbled remains of men, women, and children. Injuries to many skulls indicates that the attackers were likely members of another Bankeramik community wielding characteristic Bankeramik stone adzes, rather than the result of an attack by neighboring hunter-gatherers. This is possibly an early example of inter-village conflict.

By about 4500 BCE Bankeramik people extended across northern and central Europe all the way east to the Ukraine. Plow agriculture first appeared in the Bankeramik region by about 3600 BCE and it became widespread by about 2600 BCE. With plow agriculture fewer people were needed to work an area of land, and more land could be cleared, this is an early agricultural intensification activity. This resulted in a broader and more dispersed settlement pattern in the region and expansion into heavier soils. By this time the Bankeramik culture was organized around inherited land with powerful and prestigious individuals controlling the wealth and trade, including prestige goods.

For example, jadeite axe heads were extensively traded over long distances, perhaps as status items. Mined in the western Alps, axe heads from the same parent block have been found as far north as Scotland and Germany. Until about 4,000 BCE the people of Britain, who became isolated with the rise of sea levels at the beginning of the Holocene, had little or no significant contact with the continent. After about 4,000 BCE agriculture and continental trade goods appear in the British Isles, and perhaps some Bankeramik people themselves (or their descendants, more later).

The Megaliths and Henges

by about 4,500 BCE some French farming communities were constructing large communal stone tombs, knows as megaliths. The megaliths are found as far north as Scandinavia and as far south as Corsica and Malta in the western Mediterranean. Other later Neolithic structures include circular "henges" made of wood or stone. Stonehenge, Avebury, and Woodhenge are three examples. Dolmens, which generally consist of three large upright stones capped by a fourth stone, also appear over the landscape in the early Neolithic (Balter 2014c).

Some locations have features linked to key seasonal events, such as the solstice and equinox. The changing of the seasons would have great important for these early agricultural communities and that the intentional layout of many of these megalithic stone structures demonstrates this link, both to the changing of the seasons and to the land of their ancestors (Holtorf 1997, Tilley 1996).

In the early twentieth century, it was thought that the Megaliths were built because of contact with the southern Mediterranean, including Egypt, but later dating methods demonstrated that constructing the early megalithic sites in Europe predated the construction of the early pyramids of Egypt. More recently archaeologists have turned their attention to the surrounding landscape associated with the megaliths and hinges. For example, by the third millennium BCE Stonehenge and other nearby henges were part of a larger ceremonial landscape linked together by the Avon River and associated "avenues" (Bender 1998).

There are various theories about the megaliths and henges. Some consider them to be an expansion of Bankeramik longhouses, territorial markers, or symbols of kinship and continuity with the landscape. It is generally believed that their construction required elaborate planning and a large workforce, which suggests a centralized and authoritative decision-making process (Fairclough 1999).

Bell Beaker Society

From about 3500 BCE to about 2500 BCE many changes and innovations appear. By about 3000 BCE wheeled vehicles and battle axes made of copper or stone were spread widely over the region. Between about 2700 BCE and 2000 BCE hundreds of finely made ceramic bell-shaped beakers appear in graves and burial mounds. The wide distribution of the beakers suggests large interregional trade and contact across northern and western Europe. The beakers may have been used to contain wine or mead and were sometimes associated with archery equipment and occasionally with copper daggers. Also, at this time, amber trade routes extended from the Baltic sea over the Alps and into the Mediterranean.

A famous example is the grave of the Amesbury archer, who died in approximately 2470 BCE. It is one of the richest Beaker graves to have been found it Britain and contained the skeleton of a 34-45-year-old man accompanied by archery equipment. Through isotope analysis of his teeth archaeologists have determined that although he was buried in Britain he likely grew up in mainland Europe, which demonstrates high mobility (at least for some individuals) at the time.

Known as "Otzi the Iceman", a frozen human corpse was discovered in the Similaun Glacier between Austria and Italy in the early 1990's. The body was so well preserved that the hikers who came across it thought it was recent and an emergency medical team was called in. Later analysis of the body and associated materials, which included a backpack, bow and arrows, leather shoes, fur leggings, a cloak, and a copper axe, determined that he was approximately 45 years old when he died, sometime between 3350 and 3300 BCE. He was wearing an outer cape, woven from straw, similar to cloaks worn in parts of northern Italy as late as the 18th century. Ongoing investigations of Otzi have carefully analyzed his last meal, identified periods of illness by lines in his fingernails, and have recorded his tattoos in great detail. It was originally thought that he died of natural causes but later analysis located an arrowhead in his upper shoulder and a possible "parrying wound" on one hand which suggests that he was engaged in a violent conflict during his last moments (Fritz 2000).

Urnfield Culture

Beginning in about 2000 BCE local bronze industries developed in different parts of Europe. By the thirteenth century BCE the Urnfield people extended from France to Hungary in the east and Italy in the south. These were bronze age warrior-elites who used horse-drawn vehicles and sheet-metal helmets, shields, and bronze body armor. They also developed the bronze slashing-sword that was later adopted by the Romans. These socially stratified societies traded in salt and other materials and local monopolies were likely concentrated in the hands of comparatively few elite individuals.

By about 900 BCE agricultural production was very sophisticated. Besides plow agriculture, farmers employed field fallowing, crop rotation, and manuring to increase the productivity of different cereal and root crops.

Ironworking and Later Cultures

By the first millennium BCE ironworking techniques spread rapidly. Iron ore is found more readily that bronze and tin in the region and is much cheaper, although it is more difficult to smelt and work than bronze it is much more useful for both weapons and utilitarian purposes.

At about this time a nomadic group known as the Scythians first appear on the Russian Steppes in eastern Europe. They lived in felt tents and subsisted mostly on horse's milk and cheese and food from hunting and fishing. Their burials contain fragments of woven rugs, which are among the earliest examples in the world. The Scythian influence on Europe is still being debated.

The Hallstatt culture is thought to have developed out of the earlier Urnfield culture and spread widely through Europe. They engaged in trade with the Mediterranean up the Rhine River and through the Alps. Their villages were usually fortified.

By the fifth century BCE the La Tene Culture had developed in the Rhine and Danube river valleys. They employed elaborately worked implements and weapons in bronze and gold. Their art seems to have roots in Greek and Mediterranean traditions although their technology was a specific adaptation to woodland Europe. Their villages were fortified, some regions developed coinage, and may have been developing small states when Julius Caesar and his Roman soldiers arrived between 58-51 BCE. These may be the people that the Romans called the Celts.

THE LONG WALK HERE

Table 5. Egypt, Saharan and Sub-Saharan Africa
Unless otherwise stated dates are the beginning or earliest dates

Approx. Lakh Time	Key Event, Time Period, or Site	Approx. Date
11:59 PM	Today	
11:58 PM	Sputnik 1, Space Age Begins	1957
11:50 PM	Portuguese Arrive	1470
11:49 PM	Great Zimbabwe	400
11:42 PM	Coastal Trade East Africa - Islam	1000
11:42 PM	Bantu Migration to South Africa	1000
11:25 PM	Roman Conquest of Egypt	30 BCE
11:20 PM	Alexander the Great Conquers Egypt	332 BCE
11:17 PM	Persian Occupation	525 BCE
11:13 PM	Nubian Pharaohs	730 BCE
11:10 PM	Ironworking	900 BCE
11:09 PM	Cereal cultivation in sub-Sahara	1,000 BCE
11:08 PM	Late Period	1,070 BCE
11:03 PM	Tutankhamun	1,332 BCE
11:00 PM	New Kingdom	1,530 BCE
10:58 PM	Second Intermediate Period	1,640 BCE
10:52 PM	Present Sahara Conditions	2,000 BCE
10:50 PM	Middle Kingdom	2,140 BCE
10:49 PM	First Intermediate Period	2,180 BCE
10:43 PM	Great Pyramid of Egypt	2,528 BCE
10:43 PM	Egypt Old Kingdom and Pyramids	2,575 BCE
10:34 PM	Egyptian State and Hieroglyphs	3,100 BCE
10:34 PM	Irrigation Agriculture	3,100 BCE
10:19 PM	Flood Agriculture established on Nile	4,000 BCE
10:10 PM	Sedentism in N Africa Established	4,500 BCE
9:46 PM	Agriculture arrives in Nile	6,000 BCE
9:37 PM	Sahara a temperate desert	6,500 BCE

11 EGYPT, SAHARAN AND SUB-SAHARAN AFRICA

Regional Overview

Africa is the second-largest continent on the planet yet, outside of Egypt, it is probably one of the least understood from an archaeological perspective. The climatic zones and vegetation extend from coastal to montane and from desert to rainforest. Most zones run horizontally (east-west) when viewed from a map with the large Sahara Desert occupying the northern 1/3 of the continent and the lush Nile River Valley running from its origins Ethiopia (White Nile) and Tanzania (Blue Nile) north in a roughly 3,000-mile-long journey into the Mediterranean. For most of its journey it cuts a deep gorge in the desert. It is almost poetic that one of the oldest civilizations in the world (Egypt) is fed by waters that partly originate near the Great Rift Valley in eastern Africa, the "point of origin" for all of humanity (discussed earlier).

Saharan and Sub Saharan Africa

Since the beginning of the Holocene many changes have occurred in the Sahara in North Africa. At about 10,000 BCE it was much like it is today but by about 6500 BCE humidity had increased and the region was a temperate desert in the north with grasslands and dry savanna to the south. Beginning about 2000 BCE present arid conditions largely prevailed Connah 2013).

Several sites in North Africa have produced pottery dating to about 9,400 BCE, making it the location of some of the oldest pottery in the world.

This pottery was produced by semi-sedentary hunter-gatherers who lived near various lakes that existed in the Sahara at the time.

In about 6000 BCE severe drought conditions prevailed in Southwest Asia and some nomadic groups with goats and sheep may have crossed the Sinai into Lower Egypt, bringing barley, wheat, and sheep with them. They would have encountered hunter-gatherers along the Nile Valley. These hunter-gatherer groups may have taken up agricultural practices during this and later droughts. So, it seems that, the origins of agriculture for the Nile Valley were not a local development but were introduced from neighboring Southwest Asia.

By about 4000 BCE agriculture was well established along the Nile. Local communities depended on agriculture and relied on the annual flooding of the Nile to water their crops until about 3100 BCE when irrigation agriculture begins (and the dynastic rule of the Pharaohs). The annual flooding depended on rainfall far upstream and was not reliable enough to support the growing population. It was supplemented by irrigation as an agricultural intensification strategy that required administrative planning and control.

Cattle had been domesticated and herded in the depths of the Sahara for several millennia prior to 2000 BCE and there is evidence of sedentism in the region by about 4500 BCE. Instead of following cattle on their annual migrations, it is thought that early Saharan pastoralists prevented herds from moving long distances and unintentionally began the process of domestication.

Early farming sites in Sub-Saharan Africa were almost all north of the equator. Most of sub-Saharan Africa is home to the tsetse fly (which carries sleeping sickness) and are not suitable for raising cattle. When the Sahara dried up pastoralists with cereal crops moved south and introduced cattle herding in hospitable regions as far south as the East African highlands (Zimbabwe).

Contrary to popular belief, there are few "pure" pastoralists (a society that subsists on herding alone). It is believed that the Saharan herders who moved south to escape the drought conditions were also cultivating sorghum, millet, and other tropical rainfall crops, although there are archaeological preservation issues associated with this conclusion. Cereal cultivation in sub-Saharan Africa did not appear until the introduction of ironworking in the first millennium AD, which roughly corresponds with the Bantu migration that began in the Grassfields of Cameroon (just north of the equator) and extended through a variety of routes to encompass most of sub-Saharan Africa. This is an area of ongoing research.

By the end of the first millennium AD ironworking was being developed throughout north and central Africa. There was extensive coastal trade along east Africa. At this time this area was firmly under Islamic control. Monsoon winds linked the Red Sea with India, and also linked East Africa with Somalia and Mozambique with the larger world. Gold and ivory were obtained from southeast Africa and traded in coastal towns and villages where they were transferred to sailing ships such as the dhow.

The Portuguese arrived in western Africa in the 1470's and navigated the southern tip of Africa by 1497. Jenne-jaro was a large town at the southwestern end of the Niger Delta in West Africa that became a trading center for gold, iron, and agricultural produce. It also became an exchange point for Saharan copper and salt. Salt was in such poor supply in West Africa it traded for its equivalent weight in gold at the time. The kingdom of Ghana straddled the northern borders of the Niger and Senegal River valleys and became the center of trade for gold, ivory, kola nuts, salt and ... slaves.

During the fourteenth and fifteenth centuries, Great Zimbabwe in southern Africa now controlled most of this gold and ivory trade. Great Zimbabwe became a sizable town (maybe as large as 18,000 population) and was in part a military state, capable of raising armies from the local pastoralist population, and was also a trading center. Glass vessels from Southwest Asia, Arabic coins, and Chinese pottery have all been found there. The nation of Zimbabwe is named after this site.

Africans were later drawn into a much wider economic world fueled by demands for raw materials and for slaves. Local chiefs and warlords controlled the trade for slaves used to mine gold in Africa, to organize elephant hunting expeditions for ivory, and work the sugar and cotton plantations in the New World. In 1855 the going price in the interior of Africa for one Conus shell (that could be picked up by the dozen on coastal reefs) was one slave.

Egypt

The Egyptian state emerged in about 3100 BCE with the unification of Lower Egypt (the Nile Delta) and Upper Egypt (from the Nile Delta to Nubia, Meroe, and Aksum in the highlands of the south). It is believed that some early village farming communities acquired more wealth and more power than their neighbors. Eventually they established a monopoly over local trade and food surpluses. By being the "first to market" in this sense, they overrode any threat posed by latecomers and dominated a region (Kemp 2005).

The process of intensification in Egypt resulted from thousands of years of adjustments to the Nile floodplain environment. Key variables associated with the origins of the Egyptian State include fluctuations of the Nile (by controlling irrigation), occasional foreign influence, the personal leadership style of a divine pharaoh, and the exploitation of the common farmer by a group of hereditary elites.

By the time of the emergence of the Egyptian state there were increasing trade contacts with southwest Asia. Access to the Red Sea overland to the east was along just a few caravan routes, and trade to the west was even more restricted, with access only through a series of oases in the eastern Sahara. Egypt was effectively isolated from exterior threats for most of its early period.

The first Egyptian pharaoh was King Narmer (Menes) of the powerful village of Nekhen, sometimes called Hierankopolis. The Narmer palette, a slab of slate carved on both sides, shows King Narmer wearing the white crown of Upper Egypt and the red crown of Lower Egypt and depicts his victory over a northern ruler in about 3000 BCE. This was a symbolic linking of the gods Horus and Seth depicted in later Egyptian art.

Overall the Egyptian state existed for almost a thousand years with 31 dynasties and over 300 pharaohs. It was centrally controlled from different locations at different times through administrative districts or nomes. Each nome was headed by a hereditary nomarch whose power was exceeded only by the pharaoh. There is thought that the nomes may be rooted in the early regional villages discussed above.

Writing became fully developed in Egypt at about the same time as the formation of the first Egyptian state and reflects a tradition of deeply symbolic communication. Egyptian hieroglyphs were more than just images. They combined pictographs with phonetics, and could be read and spoken. They were not only carved on public buildings, but were also written on papyrus and painted on clay and wood. Egyptian hieroglyphs were deciphered with the discovery of the Rosetta Stone which dates to about 196 BCE. The stone itself was discovered by a French soldier during Napoleon's occupation of Egypt in 1799 and has the same message carved in Egyptian hieroglyphics, Demotic Egyptian (a cursive form of hieroglyphics), and in Ancient Greek which provided the necessary clues to decode the hieroglyphs.

The ancient Egyptian civilization is conventionally divided into four broad periods: Old Kingdom, Middle Kingdom, New Kingdom, and Persian rule which began in 525 BCE. Each of these was punctuated by an Intermediate Period. Persian Egypt was ultimately conquered by Alexander the Great in 332 BCE and by the Romans in 30 BCE.

Old Kingdom and the Pyramids (and First Intermediate Period)

From about 2575 BCE to about 2180 BCE Egypt saw four dynasties of pharaohs. During this period, Egyptian architects also experimented with different types of pyramid construction.

Egyptian pyramids served as burials for the elite and it is believed that they began with the square-block mastabas. The earliest pyramids were a series of mastabas stacked one on top of another giving the appearance of a "stepped" pyramid structure such as the early "Stepped Pyramid" of the pharaoh Djoster. Later pyramids experimented with different angles for the sides and dealt with structural issues that required architectural adjustments such as the "Collapsed Pyramid" and the "Bent Pyramid" associated with the pharaoh Seneferu. Eventually Seneferu's architects got it right with the "Red Pyramid" with a less steep angle that served as a model for later pyramids, including the famous "Great Pyramid" at Giza built by the Pharaoh Khufu in about 2528 BCE (Feder 2008:284-287, Lehner 1997).

The pyramids were usually constructed from locally quarried limestone blocks. Evidence is that at least sometimes the workers who constructed the pyramids were not slaves, as commonly depicted in the movies, but were rather skilled craftsmen who ate a superior diet, lived in comfortable barracks, and were buried in their own cemeteries. An inscription on the inside of one of the limestone blocks at the Pyramid of Khufu supports this. It reads, "We did this with pride in the name of our great King Khnum-Khuf". Much like a modern army, workers were organized into crews of 2,000, with gangs of 1,000, and so forth down to the "phyle" or "basic unit" which contained 20 workers.

The pyramids did not stand alone in the landscape; they formed a "pyramid complex" and were often surrounded by workers' villages, elaborate ceremonial buildings and roadways, and a vast network of buried materials including several boats, at least some of which were designed to be taken apart and ported to another location where they could be reassembled and launched again. Although the pyramids were primarily intended for royal burials, the associated materials provide information about many other aspects of Egyptian life. The Great Sphynx, for example, is carved from a single rock outcrop and is thought by some to pre-date the nearby pyramids because the causeway linking one notable pyramid with its associated mortuary temple is bent to go around the Sphynx. Sphynx-like images are found in both Egypt and neighboring Assyria, and later in Persia.

The pharaoh was considered a divine ruler. He (all but one were male) ruled by his own word and was considered a god. He often carried a mace and the staff of a Shepard. He had power over all people, including foreign visitors, the rainfall, and perhaps most important, over the Nile floods. He was at the apex of a highly stratified society and controlled an army of up to 20,000, many of them mercenaries.

Various skilled craftsmen rose to power during this period. One is Inty-Shedu whose life is memorialized in a series of seated sculptures in his tomb that depict him in various times of his life as the "overseer of the boat of Neith" and later as the "king's acquaintance". One of the most noticeable features of this Old Kingdom specialist is a "pencil moustache" which is still proudly worn by skilled members of the Egyptian working class in the 21st century (Hawass n.d.)

Elite male youths were encouraged to go to special schools to learn to write and become scribes. They were told, "Your limbs will be sleek … you will go forth in white clothes, honored, with courtiers saluting you." The royal bureaucracy seems to have been extensive, the "keeper of the sandals" was apparently an important role with high rank and privileges in the Old Kingdom.

This bureaucratic structure was supported by taxing the farmers on a portion their agricultural production and with their physical labor to build monuments. The agricultural harvests were carefully overseen and monitored by officials.

Political instability marked the end of the Old Kingdom in 2180 BCE. The last great Old Kingdom pharaoh, Pepi II, reigned for 94 years. After his death there may have been a succession dispute, the bureaucratic hierarchy had become top-heavy, and Egypt entered a 300-year drought. Likely a combination of these events brought a temporary end to the central rule of the pharaoh and a shift of power to a competing mosaic of small kingdoms, centered on the regional nomes (discussed earlier). The First   Intermediate

Period lasted about 40 years, from 2180 BCE to 2140 BCE and another transformation occurred which lead to the Middle Kingdom.

Middle Kingdom (and Second Intermediate Period)

In 2140 BCE Mentuhotep II founded a new dynasty in the city of Thebes, which had become the center of rebel movements earlier. The Middle Kingdom pharaohs reunited Egypt, they conquered the lands of Nubia to the south, they developed various oases to the west for agricultural purposes, and they created enormous public works and royal cemeteries, but they did not engage in the grand pyramid construction that characterized the tyrannical rulers of Old Kingdom.

The Middle Kingdom lasted until 1640 BCE when pharaonic control again weakened. The Second Intermediate Period followed and lasted nearly a thousand years, from 1640 BCE to 1530 BCE. When we think of "intermediate periods" we seldom realize that they often lasted longer than entire pharaonic periods, and sometime they lasted less than a human lifetime. Toward the end of the second intermediate period he Nile delta fell to Hyksos rulers shortly after a likely immigration from southwest Asia. The Hyksos or "foreign" rulers brought with them superior military technology, including stronger bows and the formidable horse-drawn chariot.

New Kingdom

In 1530 BCE the New Kingdom was forged when Theban rulers defeated the Hyksos rulers. Thebes was known as the "Estate of Amun" and was the home of Egypt's most powerful god. Temples to Amun were built at various locations, including Karnak. During this period the pharaoh Akhenaten created a furor by disbanding the Cult of Amun and establishing an almost monotheistic religion centered on the city of El-Amarna. Later, his son Tutankhamun re-established the cult of Amun. This period also saw the rule of the only female pharaoh, Queen Hatshepsut.

Tutankhamun's reign was short ten years. He reigned from 1332 BCE to about 1322 BCE and was apparently hastily buried in an obscure chamber in the Valley of the Kings. Due to likely flood debris that covered the entrance for millennia it was discovered in 1922 by Howard Carter in the last days of his expedition. When he opened the sealed chamber, and peered inside he was asked, "What do you see?" Carter's reported answer was, "Things, wonderful things."

The actual cause of Tutankhamun's death is highly debated as is whether or not he led his soldiers on an expedition to conquer Nubia in 1323 BCE (more later). He was succeeded by Aye, one of his key advisors who married his widow. Aye was quickly succeeded by one of Tutankhamun's generals, Horemhab, who had led military campaigns in neighboring Syria under Tutankhamun's orders. Whether his death was accidental or intentional, Tutankhamun reigned for a short period during a characteristically tumulus time (Reeves 1990).

Later pharaonic successors include Ramses II who reigned from 1279 BCE to 1273 BCE . Ramses II was one of Egypt's most powerful pharaohs and his mummy, but not his elaborate burial goods, has been recovered. The New Kingdom ended in 1070 BCE.

Late Period

The Late Period lasted from 1070 BCE to 332 BCE. During this period a series of foreign rulers conquered Egypt including the Nubian pharaohs in the eighth century BCE. The Assyrian army later occupied parts of Egypt and looted Thebes. Even later the Persians invaded and briefly occupied Egypt in 525 BCE. When Alexander the Great's army arrived in 332 BCE Ptolemaic pharaohs (of Greek ancestry) were established and they ruled until the Roman conquest in 30 BCE. This was made famous in the popular minds by the movie about the romance and power struggle between Cleopatra and would-be Roman Emperor Mark Anthony.

Complex Interactions

The Egyptian State was originally occupied by a generally Mediterranean population but illustrations in tomb paintings and biological data and imagery suggest an increasingly cosmopolitan African population in later centuries. Egypt had close ties with many other lands and peoples, including tropical Africa.

Upstream on the Nile was Nubia, which ruled Egypt briefly. Sometimes called the Land of Kush, it was famous to ancient Egyptians for its gold, ivory, and slaves. For thousands of years Egypt treated Nubia as a private reserve for human and animal game. Between 730 BCE and 663 BCE Nubian monarchs ruled Kush and Egypt itself. Meroe is a good example of this period. Meroe lies on the east bank of the White Nile, about 124 miles north of Khartoum in modern Sudan. The burial structures in Meroe resemble Egyptian pyramids and other New Kingdom tombs but were built over 800 years after the last royal pyramid was built in Egypt and have their own stylistic characteristics (taller and narrower than the wide-angle pyramids of the old kingdom).

By the first century AD the Kingdom of Aksum in Ethiopia, was in regular contact with Rome and traded through its port at Adulis on the Red Sea. In the 4th century AD, King Ezana of Aksum adopted Christianity, making Ethiopia one of the earliest Christian Kingdoms of the world, possibly earlier than the adoption of Christianity (in AD 395) by Rome under Constantine (the Ethiopian date is uncertain). Christian churches, quarried entirely into bedrock, similar to the rock-cut churches in the Levant such as Petra, are found here. In Aksum, large stelae that somewhat resemble Egyptian obelisks mark the locations of royal and other burials, some are nearly 70 feet high. The Egyptian influence on the Kush and Aksum, far up the Nile, is often not recognized in the popular mind and many people do not know that Egypt had Nubian pharaohs.

Table 6. South and Southeast Asia
Unless otherwise stated dates are the beginning or earliest dates

Approx. Lakh Time	Key Event, Time Period, or Site	Approx. Date
11:59 PM	Today	
11:58 PM	Sputnik 1 Launched, Space Age Begins	1957
11:45 PM	Angkor Thom - Cambodia	AD 1181
11:44 PM	Angkor Wat - Cambodia	AD 1113
11:39 PM	Jayaraman II – Cambodia Khmer Empire	AD 802
11:25 PM	Extensive SE Asia Sea Trade	AD 1
11:21 PM	Emperor Akosa (India)	272 BCE
11:20 PM	Mauryan Empire Begins (India)	319 BCE
11:20 PM	Alexander the Great India Campaign	326 BCE
11:09 PM	Bronze in SE Asia	1,000 BCE
11:00 PM	Ganges River Valley Development	1,500 BCE
11:00 PM	Harrapan Civilization Disappears	1,500 BCE
10:44 PM	City of Mohenjo-daro Indus Valley	2,500 BCE
10:35 PM	Farming Villages and Rice in SE Asia	3,000 BCE
10:32 PM	Harrapan Civilization Rises Indus Valley	3,200 BCE
10:19 PM	Proto-urban Towns, Kot Diji in Indus Valley	4,000 BCE
9:29 PM	Mehgarh, Domesticated cattle, barley, wheat, cotton	7,000 BCE
8:44 PM	Younger Dryas (cold snap) ends	9,650 BCE
8:23 PM	Younger Dryas (cold snap) begins	10,950 BCE
8:22 PM	Holocene Begins	11,000 BCE
7:15 PM	Glacial Maximum	15,000 BCE

12 SOUTH AND SOUTHEAST ASIA

Regional Overview

South Asia is a landmass of about 1.4 million square miles and it is home to one-fifth of the current world's population, southeast Asia is even larger. It is a melting pot of languages and religions yet little is known about the earliest developments in the region that includes portions of the modern states of India, Pakistan, and portions of Tibet. The region hosts the world's highest mountains and a vast array of river systems and coastlines.

The Indus River originates in southern Tibet and descends a thousand miles through Kashmir before flowing through the semiarid Indus Valley, which lies between Pakistan and India, and then into the Arabian Sea. The region is characterized by hot summers and sometimes cold winters. Water was obtained largely from the Indus River and some smaller neighboring rivers and streams.

Harrapan Civilization (India)

Hemmed in by mountains, South Asia developed its own preindustrial civilization that was unknown to the modern world until it was discovered by Sir John Marshall, in the early twentieth century. He once boasted that he left India 2,000 years older than he found it. The early inhabitants were hunter-gatherers who spent their summers in the mountains and winters in the plains near the rivers and by about 7000 BCE there is evidence of early agriculture.

Mehgarh, in western Pakistan, which dates to the seventh millennium BCE, is a small pre-pottery settlement with various mud-brick compartments, possibly used for storing grain. Besides domesticating zebu cattle, the inhabitants of Mehgarh may have raised barley, wheat, and possibly rice. They may also have been among the earliest people to domesticate cotton. By about 4000 BCE we see proto-urban towns such as Kot Diji that may have their origins in earlier Neolithic communities like Mehgarh.

From evidence like this it is believed that the Harrapan Civilization developed independently, perhaps as the result of complex maritime and overland trade and exchange networks in the region (both east to central Asia and west to then Sumaria).

The Harrapan Civilization's origins date to about 3200 BCE, it reached its peak at about 2000 BCE and by 1000 BCE it had disappeared. Remember, archaeologists define "civilization" as an urbanized state-level society. It flourished along the Indus River for a few hundred years before vanishing from the face of the earth only to be re-discovered just over three thousand years later. Much about the origin, fluorescence, and disappearance of this civilization remains a mystery. The process has been referred to as a "paroxysm of change" (Conningham 2013, McIntosh 2008, Possehl 2003).

Mohenjo-daro

Excavations at Mohenjo-daro, dating to 2500 BCE, have raised more questions than they have provided answers and suggest a possible link or migration to the Ganges. Possible priest-kings are depicted in sculptures wearing garments with one shoulder uncovered. This was a sign of reverence during Buddha's life, more than one thousand years later along the Ganges river and a thousand miles to the east. They also wore headbands with hollow circular orbs on the forehead. Female dancing figurines, sculptures of boats and wheeled vehicles are also present. There was also a script, of sorts (largely on seals like the one discussed below), but it has not been deciphered (Conningham 2013).

Did they have bombastic rulers boasting of their achievements on "grandiose palace walls"? No. there is very little, if any, evidence of endemic warfare and conquest. We need more data but Mohenjo-daro also boasted a "great bath" that was the only free-standing structure in the city which could be accessed from the outside. This evidence suggests a strong focus on "lustration" or some ceremonial or ritual bathing (Jansen 1989).

A seal from Mohenjo-daro depicts a three-headed figure who sits in the yogic posture and wears a horned headdress. A tiger, an elephant, a rhinoceros, a water buffalo, and a deer surround him. This, to some, strongly suggests the iconography associated with the later Hindu god Siva and a relationship with later Hindu beliefs.

Harappa

Harappa was an urban city with scores of smaller satellite settlements in the Indus Valley. It dates to about 2600 BCE and is the namesake for that is known as the Harrapan Civilization. It was a carefully planned city and domestic apartments with wells for water, an urban sewer system, and even what may be personal shower stalls. This suggests a stratified society with centralized government. But, like their forbearers, we cannot decipher their script and we are left wondering about the names of their rulers and the types of trade they engaged in.

Clearly there were no bombastic rulers who carved images of themselves smiting their enemies (as we saw to the west in Mesopotamia). The self-glorification of rulers so characteristic of Egypt, Syria, and Assyria during the same time is absent here. The Harrapans traded with Sumeria, because we find Sumerian artifacts in Harrapan cities and Harrapan materials in Sumerian cities. They could not conceivably have been oblivious to Sumerian warfare but for some reason did not seem to emulate it. We find symmetrical granaries for storing agricultural produce. Again, that suggests a centralized planning and construction system. But we find little associated with the typical hereditary control associated with warrior priest-kings.

Decline

Some scholars suggest that Indo-European peoples from the north (often called Aryans) spread into the region during the second millennium BCE and conquered and then intermarried with the local population. This is a diffusionist perspective. Other scholars suggest there was no invasion and that the developments were entirely indigenous. This is a local innovation perspective.

One piece of evidence relating to this perspective is the "Mojenjo'daro Massacre". When originally excavated, this pit of sprawled skeletons was interpreted as evidence of warfare and conquest. It was later interpreted as a peaceful, but hasty, mass burial, complete with grave goods and no signs of violence (Dales 1964).

Were the people hastily buried due to an epidemic? We don't' know. Is there other evidence of conflict? Yes. There are several instances where it appears that a few individuals were killed in what may have been a hasty retreat. Until more excavations occur, we simply will not know the answers to these many questions.

Ganges River Valley

After the disappearance of the Harrapan civilization in the Indus Valley at about 1500 BCE there was increased activity in the Ganges River Valley to the east. Various local rulers later controlled different areas of what is now India and Pakistan. Hinduism and Buddhism both trace their origins to this vast period. After about 521 BCE the Persian Empire under Darius expanded into the Indus River Valley (but not to the Ganges). In 326 BCE Alexander The Great began his Indian campaign. Two years after his death, in 321 BCE, the Mauryan Empire was founded by Chandragupta Maurya.

Later, emperor Asoka, who ruled from 235-272 BCE, left a lasting mark. Majestic pillars capped with lions were erected by him throughout his empire with inscriptions saying, "Forsake violence and greed, show reverence for animals, establish works of public benefit, rectify bureaucracy and other administrative evils". Akosa led a state that depended on militaristic control, and yet he was also a philosopher who questioned the morality of militarism. When India became a republic in 1950, the national emblem was based on Asoka's pillars that by then were nearly 1,700 years old.

Southeast Asia

There are three major river systems in Southeast Asia. This is the area we know today as Cambodia, Laos, Thailand, and Vietnam, generally. These rivers hosted their own complex societies for many centuries. These rivers generally run from the north to the south, including the Mekong River which runs from China through Southeast Asia to the Pacific Ocean. Later developments in the region followed these rivers, including the introduction of rice farming (likely from China) with rice as the staple crop. By the third millennium BCE village life seems well established.

The transition from hunting and gathering to sedentary village farming life probably spread from the Yangzi River Valley south and to the west. This is paralleled by the distribution of what is called Austroasiatic languages that are found today from eastern India, to southern China, and to some islands in the Pacific. Using linguistic tools, which are becoming much more sophisticated lately – but in association with genetic evidence, archaeologists are slowly uncovering many mysteries of this region.

It is only within the past two millennia we see evidence of high populations in Southeast Asia. The environment is dependent on monsoon cycles and complex societies were topographically limited to fertile enclaves. One example is Dong Son, in Vietnam's Red River Valley. Indigenous origins reach to at least about 1,000 BCE where two rice crops a year could be produced, and where bronze working became very important.

Seafarers and sea trade were also important to this region. By about AD 1 the sea trading networks of Southeast Asia were established. Sea trade extended to India, with a profound influence on the region, and to China and to the Romans in the far west.

By the end of the first millennium BCE, highly stratified centralized kingdoms with an elite class appear in the region. There was a strong cultural connection with ancestors and these rulers invoked divine status, often associated with the Hindu god Siva. These kingdoms dotted the landscape from the lower and middle Mekong Valley to the Vietnamese coastal plain.

Khmer Empire

As we have seen elsewhere, eventually regional conflicts led to one warlord coming to power. In about AD 802 Jayaraman II (of present day Cambodia) conquered neighboring areas and established them up as tribute kingdoms. First "discovered" by Westerners in the 1860's this may be the regions' first civilization. Angkor Wat is one of the world's largest religious monuments and dates to a little later, about AD 1113. It serves as the temple mausoleum of King Suryavarman II of Angkor. The central temple at Angkor Wat was built with the solar calendar in mind. It measures 365 "hat" in length and width (one "hat" equals 1.43 feet). The spring equinox sun rises directly over the central lotus tower.

In about AD 1181 Jayavarman VII, a Buddhist, built Angkor Thom in Cambodia as his capitol near Angkor Wat. This complex was abandoned in AD 1431. The Bayon at Angkor Wat is a world-famous temple-mausoleum that is thought to represent the king as a bodhisattva from the Buddhist tradition. Images at Angkor Thom depicts a fierce battle between Jayavarman VII and neighboring forces. It is believed that his ashes were scattered below the central tower. It is speculated that perhaps a million people once lived in or near Angkor Thom. One temple, at nearby Angkor Wat, contains at least 430 images, and an inscription nearby boasts that 306,372-people worked on building the shrine.

Although much remains to be discovered, the ancient archipelago of Southeast Asia became a mixing ground of peoples and ideas beginning with *Homo erectus* (much earlier from Africa) and more recently from India to the west and China to the north. The region's climate, topography, and river systems all contributed to a complex mosaic of cultural exchange that is only now beginning to be understood.

THE LONG WALK HERE

Table 7. China and Central and East Asia
Unless otherwise stated dates are the beginning or earliest dates

Approx. Lakh Time	Key Event, Time Period, or Site	Approx. Date
11:59 PM	Today	
11:58 PM	Sputnik 1 Launched, Space Age Begins	1957
11:46 PM	Mongol Empire	1215
11:22 PM	Han Dynasty	206 BCE
11:22 PM	Unification under Qin	221 BCE
11:20 PM	Jomon – Japan – Ends	300 BCE
11:16 PM	Confucius	551 BCE
11:07 PM	Zhou Dynasty	1,122 BCE
11:06 PM	Shang Dynasty	1,150 BCE
10:54 PM	States Appear – Bronze, Erlitou, (Xia Dynasty?)	1,900 BCE
10:52 PM	Earliest Millet Noodles in Arch. Record, bronze	2,000 BCE
10:35 PM	Longshan – Fortifications	3,000 BCE
10:31 PM	Liangzu – Early Writing (scapula)	3,250 BCE
10:19 PM	Longshan Arises - Elites	4,000 BCE
10:02 PM	Yangshao – Millet Farmers	5,000 BCE
9:37 PM	Village Farming in Northern China	6,500 BCE
9:29 PM	Rice Cultivation Well Established	7,000 BCE
9:12 PM	Rice Cultivation Begins	8,000 BCE
8:44 PM	Younger Dryas (cold snap) Ends	9,650 BCE
8:39 PM	Wild Rice Harvesting	10,000 BCE
8:23 PM	Younger Dryas (cold snap) Begins	10,950 BCE
8:22 PM	Holocene Begins	11,000 BCE
7:57 PM	Jomon Pottery (Japan)	12,500 BCE
7:15 PM	Glacial Maximum	15,000 BCE

13 CHINA AND CENTRAL AND EAST ASIA

Regional Overview

China and Central and East Asia is a very large geographic area with several environmental zones including large coastal areas, inland forests, mountain steppes, mountains, and deserts in the northern latitudes. Two major river systems dominate this vast region, the Yellow River (to the North) and the Yangtze River (to the South). The country known as China is the third largest in the world at about 3.7 million square miles (behind only Russia and Canada).

Early Farming in China

The early farming cultures in China were centered on both the Yellow River and Yangzi River and key lakes and coastal areas. Wild rice is a marsh plant and cultivating it requires recreating marshy conditions. The plant feeds on blue-green algae that circulates past the plant. Drought conditions and dry spells can be disastrous for rice producers.

Wild rice was being exploited as early as about 10,000 BCE and by about 7000 BCE it was well-established as a cultivated crop. Early Holocene conditions in the cave of Diaotonghuan reveal abundant wild rice phytoliths (microscopic silica structures found inside plants that can identify a species) but when the Younger Dryas (mentioned earlier) occurred there were relatively few. By the full onset of the current warm phase (discussed earlier) we see the reappearance of rice phytoliths in abundance and pottery. Rice became so important that today it accounts for over 20% of the total calories consumed by all humans worldwide.

Village farming life was well-established in both northern and southern China by about 6500 BCE although millet was the staple in the north and rice was the staple in the south.

The Yangshao culture, dating to about 5000 BCE, is probably the best known of China's early millet farming people. Millet is a fast-growing cereal plant that can be produced in poor soils and cooler environments. Millet likely originated in the eastern borders of the Himalaya Mountains. When domesticated it requires shallow water. It produces small seeds that can be ground into flour or used for fermentation. Today, millet is often sold as food for domesticated birds. Yangshao villages are generally found on terraces in the Yellow River Basin where the fertile soil could be tilled using hoes and digging sticks. Yangshao villages were typically surrounded by deep ditches that protected the residences within.

By about 3000 BCE the Yangshao were replaced by Longshan farming cultures in northern China. Their settlements were larger than Yangshao and often protected by earthen walls. We see the appearance of more complex ranked societies and more advanced agricultural technology. There is a variety of pottery and also pottery containers for alcohol.

Chinese Civilization

By about 4000 BCE population densities had risen throughout the region due to the expansion of rice farming and millet farming. Irrigation of rice crops was widespread. The oldest millet noodles (and they look like noodles today) date to about 2000 BCE and were found at the site of Lajia in northwestern China. Millet is truly a late Neolithic staple in the region, as is rice.

The Chinese Longshan tradition (mentioned earlier) arose about 4000 BCE in both north and south China where villages were interlinked by complex exchange networks, including both commodities and elite goods. This network eventually grew to define some of the interior territorial boundaries that affected later Chinese civilization.

By about 3250 BCE the later Liangzu culture had developed in the Shanghai Delta area. It is characterized by prestigious burials that indicate a highly stratified society where extreme wealth and prestige marked the rulers, and separated them from the commoners who produced the agricultural surplus.

Writing

Cracked ox shoulder blades (scapula) from this period often have inscriptions on them that suggest they were used in divination ceremonies. Earlier Neolithic cracked tortoise shells are also often associated with an even number of black and white stones, suggesting, perhaps, the origins of the popular western board game "Chinese checkers". These shells also contain inscriptions that suggest divination.

It is thought that modern Chinese writing may have originated from divination ceremonies. The modern phonetic images may have their origins in earlier pictographic representations. The similarities between many early images and the modern simplified script are very strong, the image for "sun" for example, on early oracle bones was a circle with a horizontal line in it, the modern image is a stylized rectangle bisected by a horizontal line.

Unlike Mesopotamia, where writing seems to have originated from accounting and record- keeping. Writing in China seems to have its origins in a more futuristic purpose, perhaps relating to learning in advance the prospects of various military expeditions, or marriage alliances among the elite. Before we dismiss divination it as superstitious it would serve us well to remember that any investment banker, politician, or doting mother or father would pay a hefty price for even a brief glimpse into future events.

Erlitou, Xia, and the Seven Capitols

The rise of states in China dates to about 1,900 BCE with the appearance of the city of Erlitou. At the time it was the largest city in China, measuring about 300 hectares (600 football fields) and lasted until about 1,500 BCE. It contains one of the earliest palace structures in China with elite graves and bronze weaponry and vessels. Bronze working developed in China independently from the West before about 2000 BCE.

The oracle bones of the time suggest that local chieftains occupied at least seven capitols along the Yellow river, in the modern provinces of Henan, Shandong, and Anhui. These were walled towns that enjoyed similar levels of prosperity. The early rulers came to power after generations of strife with neighboring groups. The ruling elites would have likely formed independent lineages that were interwoven through allegiances and marriage.

The Xia and Shang dynasties are two early examples from this time and Erlitou may have been a Xia city. It was the center of a strongly centralized chiefdom but whether it was a true state is still debated.

Shang Dynasty

Little is known of the Xia but more is known about the Shang. The Shang ruled their province from about 1500 BCE to about 1122 BCE. The Shang were famous for their bronze work which was a guarded monopoly of the rulers. Jade was also clearly prized and often intricately worked into figures such as dragons and birds.

The royal burials often contained the remains of the king with intricately worked bronze containers and items. The royal burials were surrounded by hundreds, and sometimes thousands of lesser burials with between two and eleven people in a single tomb. Some burials were clearly sacrificial, with beheaded bodies often buried side-by-side together. One royal Shang tomb contains an entire chariot along with the supine skeletons of two horses at the front and the body of the charioteer at the rear.

The Shang city of Zhengzhou was surrounded by walls 118 feet wide at the base and still reach a height of 33 feet in places. The palace precinct is inside the walls and bronze foundries, workshops, residential areas, and burial areas are found scattered outside the city walls.

The Shang dynast fell in about 1122 BCE to their neighbors, the Zhou. The Zhou divided their realm into independent provinces which warred with one another for centuries. Early Chinese rulers were supported by strong standing armies that could be supplemented with thousands of peasant conscripts on short notice. In a sense, each early Chinese state was a fully armed garrison with armies numbering at least 10,000.

Warring States Period and Confucius

By the fifth century BCE China was controlled by at least seven competing states, each with its own hereditary dynasty, elites, and standing army. Zhou authority was in the decline and, after centuries of raw militaristic conquest a new philosophy was developing under various scholarly nobles, including Confucius (born in 551 BCE). This philosophy advocated the concept of "ru" which meant that leaders derived their power and moral authority through noble behavior, not only through ancestor worship and brute force. A noble leader would be one who excelled in the "six arts" which were calligraphy, history, poetry, archery, ritual, and music.

Confucian philosophy was never completely accepted by the ruling elites but its legacy survives today.

Unification

In 221 BCE the Qin emperor Zheng (Shi Huangdi) conquered the seven continuously warring Zhou states and unified China into a single empire. He founded the Qin dynasty, which is pronounced "Chin" and for which China is named. His dynasty lasted from 221 BCE to 207 BCE (14 years). After Shi Huangdi's death a succession dispute arose between two of his sons (and lesser nobles) and the dynasty fell. It was replaced by the Han Dynasty which reigned from 206 BCE to AD 220. The Han Dynasty was a period of enhanced central administration and geographic expansion.

The Qin dynasty is known for the royal tomb of Shi Huangdi, which has been only partly excavated. It contains an entire army of approximately 8,000 life-sized terra-cotta soldiers, each with unique facial features. An intricately worked half-size bronze carriage, drawn by four horses was discovered there and is said to be one of the finest bronzes ever discovered in China. Although thought to have been partly looted in 206 BCE the royal tomb of Shi Huangdi has never been completely excavated.

During his brief reign as the first Chinese emperor Shi Huangdi invested countless man-hours and other resources in the construction and expansion of the Great Wall which separated the agrarian economies of the central regions from the raiding nomadic-pastoralists of the north. Later dynasties would expand the Great Wall thousands of miles across China's northern border (Higham 203).

Silk Road

The silk road was not one road but a series of overland and seafaring routes linking the eastern Mediterranean Romans with China and the Pacific. It connected the two great empires of the time and served as a vehicle for the exchange of commodities, luxury goods, ideas, and also possibly certain communicable diseases such as severe plagues which occurred in Asia and northern Africa at the time. It is best known through the journals of the trader Marco Polo.

Early Agriculture in Japan

The indigenous Jomon of Japan were sedentary hunter-gatherers who subsisted primarily on shellfish and other marine resources. They produced some of the earliest pottery in the world and lasted as an identifiable culture in the archaeological record from about 12,500 BCE (possibly earlier) to about 300 BCE, just six hundred years before Japan was unified into a single state. As time progressed the pottery styles became more complex, and the bases evolved from round to flat. Later Japanese agriculturalists include the Yayoi, whose villages were generally protected by defensive ditches and tall watchtowers.

Mongol Empire

The Mongol empire was an empire of nomadic pastoralists, not sedentary agriculturalists, and it was the largest empire (in terms of square miles) in the history of the world covering nearly 2.3 million square miles. It was created by Genghis Khan. His descendants ruled over China, Tibet, Iran, much of the Near East, and Russia. The initial phase of the Mongol conquest ranged between AD 1215 and AD 1241 and persisted in places (such as Georgia) until AD 1505. Mongol warriors were expert horsemen (and women) whose battle strategy was based on ancient animal hunting methods. This was an aggressive militaristic empire with centralized leadership and symbolism (Fitzhugh et al. 2009).

THE LONG WALK HERE

Table 8. Australia and the Pacific
Unless otherwise stated dates are the beginning or earliest dates

Approx. Lakh Time	Key Event, Time Period, or Site	Key Dates
11:59 PM	Today	
11:58 PM	Sputnik 1 Launched, Space Age Begins	1957
11:55 PM	British Settle Australia as Penal Colony	1788
11:47 PM	New Zealand Colonized	1280
11:46 PM	Hawaii Colonized	1220
11:45 PM	Easter Island Colonized	1200
11:45 PM	Marquis Islands Colonized	1200
11:42 PM	Society Islands Colonized	1025
11:18 PM	Cooling in Australia	450 BCE
11:05 PM	Rice in Philippines	1,200 BCE
10:59 PM	Lapita Culture Appears	1,550 BCE
10:44 PM	Taro Cultivation in Pacific	2,500 BCE
10:27 PM	Rice in Taiwan	3,500 BCE
1:42 PM	New Guinea Settled	35,000 YA
11:30 AM	First Humans to Australia	45,000 YA

14 AUSTRALIA AND THE PACIFIC

Regional Overview

The story of human colonization of this region extends to long before the peak of the last glacial maximum (in the Northern Hemisphere) when the first humans reached Australia, approximately 50,000 years ago to as recently as about AD 1280, when the first humans reached New Zealand. It is a story of seafaring and nautical technology because none of these locations could have been reached without some watercraft. It is also a story of trade because the island resources were often limited and vital utilitarian items, such as clay for pottery and obsidian for tools, were transported and traded over hundreds and sometime thousands of miles of ocean.

The area known as Oceania in the Pacific Ocean is divided into three large island groups which are Melanesia in the southwest (this includes New Guinea), Micronesia in the northwest (which is just east of the Philippines), and Polynesia in the east (which includes New Zealand, Hawaii, and Easter Island.

Rice cultivation in Taiwan dates to about 3,500 BCE and is found in the Philippines by about 1,200 BCE. Other crops, like the root crop taro, were more adapted to the tropical and island environment and served as staples in the Philippines and Borneo and beyond. Small animals such as pigs and chickens could have been transported from island to island in single and more stable double-hulled canoes, as could plant staples such as yams and taro (Bellwood and Hiscock 2013).

The Last Diaspora

Taiwan is thought to be the "starting point" for much of the nautical colonization of the Pacific because formative versions of the Austronesian languages can be traced there. We are fortunate that linguistic studies in this region can aid the archaeological studies, because so much of the activity is very recent (relatively speaking). Major subgroups of this language are found in the Philippines and Indonesia and across the Pacific to Easter Island. The Western Malayo-Polynesian subgroup is also found across the Indian Ocean on the island of Madagascar, which is just off the eastern coast of Africa (and which supports the idea of very long nautical voyaging).

Lapita Culture

From about 1550 BCE to about 1000 BCE (over a period of nearly six centuries) the Lapita people colonized hundreds of islands across thousands of miles of ocean in Melanesia from New Britain (off the coast of New Guinea) to Samoa and Tonga. They are known for their characteristic dentate-stamped pottery. Also knows as "tattooed" pottery, the designs were meticulously stamped or inscribed into the wet pottery with a pointed instrument and have an eerie resemblance to later Maori tattoo designs in New Zealand. Lapita origins may have been from earlier Neolithic sites in Taiwan and the Philippines where similar, but older, pottery designs have been found.

Movement and trade was not simply from the west to the east, some activity was to the east from the west. Obsidian from the Bismarck Islands has been found thousands of miles to the west near Borneo. Pigs, dogs, and chickens likely came into the region from southeast Asia. Intricate bone fish hooks have been found at Lapita sites, and would likely have been carved with imported obsidian.

Eastern Polynesia

The colonization of Eastern Polynesia from the west was punctuated by several centuries where no eastward movement occurred. This may have been due to changes in the ocean currents or to changes in the trade winds, or both. A wave of canoes arrived in the Society Islands between about AD 1025 and 1121. By about AD 1200 voyagers reached the Marquesas, between about AD 1200 and 1263 they reached Rapa Nui (Eastern Island), between about AD 1219 and 1269 they reached Hawaii, and between AD 1230 and 1280 they reached New Zealand. It is thought that a primary reason for inter-island colonization may be due to population pressures in the settled islands and the desire for younger members to find new islands and to start their own lineages.

Easter Island

Rapa Nui is famous for the 900 or so moai statutes depicting human forms from the waist up, with elaborate head gear. It is also a classic example of humans over-exploiting an environment to the point of near catastrophe. It is thought by some that the stone "moai" from Rapa Nui bear a resemblance to the wooden "marae" found on Raiatea Island near Tahiti. The similarity in form and pronunciation supports the west to east migration theory. Although inconclusive some limited stonework on Rapa Nui appears to be characteristic of the Imperial Inca style. This suggests possible contact with the mainland to the west. The coast of South America is approximately 2,000 miles to the west of Rapa Nui and the island today is controlled by Chile.

Hawaii

The archipelago of islands that form Hawaii were settled by AD 1269 (and possibly as early as AD 400 by Lapita seafarers. The early colonists founded small ranked groups headed by the descendants of the leaders. Later the islands were controlled by large stratified chiefdoms that built massive dry-stone terraced religious structures and engaged in inter-island conflict and warfare. Although unclear at this time, it is possible that political unification under an archaic state may have occurred, at least for a time, prior to the arrival of the Europeans in the eighteenth century (Kirch 2010).

New Zealand

The two islands that form New Zealand were likely first settled between about AD 1230 and 1280. The island is temperate (not tropical as is typical of most of Oceania) in climate and the northern areas are warmer than the southern regions. The earliest inhabitants encountered large flightless birds called Moa which were quickly hunted to extinction (McGlone 2012). When Europeans arrived they encountered fortified Maori villages that were engaged in brutal inter-village conflict. The Maori warriors, and war canoes, were so fierce that it was several centuries before they were subdued by the Europeans. It is believed that ritual cannibalism in the region may have developed to supplement a diet poor in protein.

James Cook's Voyages

Between AD 1768 and 1779) the British captain James Cook made three voyages into the Pacific, which was claimed, but not well defended, by Spain at the time. Cook's first voyage, on Her Majesties' Sailing Ship "Endeavor" was a three-year mission to explore uncharted regions and make new discoveries. It was primarily a voyage of scientific exploration but it also included a military contingent. Cook's official purpose was to land in Tahiti and map the transit of Venus across the sun to provide measurements for the British Academy of Sciences which could help determine the distance of the Earth from the Sun (this was a major global undertaking at the time). Cook was also charged to find the rumored "Southern Continent" (later known as Antarctica), to test a prototype clock that required no pendulum and could aid seafarers in navigation, to create nautical maps of the lands he encountered (some of which are so detailed that they are reportedly still in use today), and to locate the rumored "northern passage" across North America, but this time from the west (not the east).

During his three voyages he became the first European to chart the eastern coast of Australia (where he was briefly shipwrecked on the Great Barrier Reef) and he "discovered" Hawaii. When he first landed in Hawaii he was greeted as a god because he had the good fortune to arrive in just the right season from just the right direction, that Hawaiian legend said the god Lono would return from. The native Hawaiians quickly discovered that he was not a god and on a later visit Cook was killed in a skirmish and his body was cut into pieces and scattered among the villages as either a war trophy or as a sacred talisman (as if he was indeed a god or a semi-god). Cook's second-in-command was able to retrieve most of his captain's remains and Cook was buried at sea.

While at the helm, Cook was meticulous about cleanliness on his ship and also required his crew to eat sauerkraut (which they reportedly despised) and fruits and vegetables. As a result the scourge of nautical travel "scurvy" was not present on any of his voyages, although it killed hundreds of sailors on other European sailing voyages. Some of his officers forged their own names in Pacific maritime history including Captains Vancouver and Bligh. Because of Cook's meticulous recordkeeping, and that of the naturalists on his voyages, the record of "first contact" with many Oceanic peoples is well document and assists scholars to this day (see Kirch 2010).

Australia and New Guinea

Australia and New Guinea were connected as one landmass during the glacial maximum of the Pleistocene because sea levels were at least 300 feet below the present sea level. Despite the lower sea level, the combined landmass, called Sahul, was separated from Southeast Asia by at least 50 miles of open water across the Wallacea Straight.

The earliest colonists of Sahul had to have reached it on some sort of sailing craft and did so between about 45,000 and 50,000 years ago. Much of the record of coastal activities in this region at this time lies under about 300 feet of ocean, although some modern coastlines are similar to those of the Pleistocene because of steep drop offs into the ocean. Tasmania and other areas once connected to the continent became islands by about 10,000 years ago.

There are two theories about how the early occupants spread out over the continent. One is a coastal adaptation model and the other is one of rapid cross-continental movement following migratory fauna. Although there were periods of dramatic climatic change, many aspects of Australian lithic technology remained similar for long periods of time. For example, the same stone toolmaking process used about 20,000 years ago was being used as late as 500 years ago.

At the beginning of the Holocene, with increased temperatures and precipitation, much of the continent was covered with dense forests. By about 2,500 years ago the climate became cooler, drier, and more variable. Specialized regional stone toolkits and hunting and gathering strategies developed. During the last 20,000 years a rich tradition of rock art also developed, particularly along the north coast, and some of the oldest rock art in the world can be found there. The "Rainbow Serpent", a powerful creation deity representing increased dependence on marine resources can be traced to this period.

The first British settlers in AD 1788 marked the beginning of the end of Australian prehistory and a period of rapid population decline for the native people due to disease and other factors.

New Guinea was settled by late Ice Age seafarers as early as about 35,000 BCE. The Solomon Islands and the Bismarck Archipelago was also settled at this time. Agricultural systems that cultivated taro, yams, and fruit trees such as bananas developed independently in New Guinea. By about 2500 BCE these crops were being grown throughout much of Melanesia.

THE LONG WALK HERE

Table 9. North America
Unless otherwise stated dates are the beginning or earliest dates

Approx. Lakh Time	Key Event, Time Period, or Site	Approx. Date
11:59 PM	Today	
11:58 PM	Sputnik 1 Launched, Space Age Begins	1957
11:51 PM	Historic Period Generally Begins	1525
11:51 PM	Protohistoric Period Generally Begins	1550
11:50 PM	Columbus Arrives in Caribbean	1492
11:44 PM	Mesa Verde	1130
11:44 PM	Hohokam Culture	1100
11:43 PM	Chaco Phenomenon	1050
11:43 PM	Cahokia	1050
11:42 PM	Norse Settlement in Newfoundland	1000
11:25 PM	Anasazi (Ancestral Puebloans)	1
11:25 PM	Hopewell Mounds	1
11:25 PM	Formative Period Generally Begins	1
11:20 PM	Mogollon Culture	300 BCE
11:14 PM	Adena Mounds	700 BCE
11:12 PM	Mississippian Mounds	800 BCE
11:09 PM	Maize Arrives in SE North America	1,000 BCE
11:05 PM	Koster Occupation Ends	1,200 BCE
10:52 PM	Cultivation in North America	2,000 BCE
10:49 PM	Poverty Point Culture	2,200 BCE
10:44 PM	Late Archaic Period Generally Begins	2,500 BCE
10:19 PM	Sedentary Hunter-Gatherers in Pacific NW	4,000 BCE
10:19 PM	Middle Archaic Period Generally Begins	4,000 BCE
9:29 PM	Inuit and Aleut in Arctic	7,000 BCE
9:20 PM	Koster Occupation Begins	7,500 BCE
8:47 PM	Early Archaic Period Generally Begins	9,500 BCE
8:19 PM	Clovis Big Game Hunters	11,200 BCE
8:06 PM	Paleoindian Period Generally Begins	12,000 BCE
7:00 PM	Possible Earliest Humans Arrive America	16,000 BCE

15 NORTH AMERICA

Regional Overview

The North American region extends from the frigid arctic of the north pole to the hot deserts of the Southwest and is bounded on the east by the Atlantic Ocean and the west by the Pacific Ocean. The environmental diversity is extensive and some of the most productive areas were coastlines and river valleys. At the time of European arrival thick forests covered the eastern region. These gradually gave way to the vast grasslands west of the Mississippi River. The Rocky Mountains and the Sierra Nevada Mountains, separated by the Great Basin, shape the western portion of the region. The region is commonly divided into several cultural areas with their own trajectories through time: Eastern Woodlands, The Mississippi River, the Plains, the Southwest, California, the Pacific Northwest Coast, and the Arctic.

During the Paleolithic period large megafauna such as the mammoth, mastodon, horse, and camel, which all later became extinct, shared the region with the earliest human occupants. Large herds of bison roamed the plains. Deer and antelope were a mainstay for hides and meat. Turkey, hare/rabbit and many other mammals were also present. Native plants included tobacco and over 30,000 plant varieties including seed grasses (chenopods), nut producing trees, fruits, and berries. Maritime resources such as salmon were particularly important in the Pacific Northwest. Dogs were the only domesticated animal species until the domestication of the wild Turkey at about the time that maize agriculture was introduced from Central America.

Paleolithic Period

There is no conclusive evidence of any human occupation of the continent prior to the last 18,000 years, during the last Glacial Maximum of the Pleistocene, although the time and method of human colonization of the continent is a matter of much debate. A terrestrial route across Beringia and south through a hypothetical ice-free corridor between two large ice sheets is the most likely scenario. During the last ice age this land bridge (Beringia) would have connected Siberia and Alaska due to low sea levels.

Another scenario is a coastal migration using water craft along the Pacific Rim that exploited the coastal and inland resources. Linguistic, genetic, and morphological evidence strongly support Eastern Asia as the source population although when this occurred and whether or not it occurred in one wave or in three is not clear. For example, sinodonty is a pattern of dental morphology that includes shovel shaped incisors characteristic of many Amerindian populations as far south as South America. These characteristics can also be found in modern Mongolian and Siberian populations.

A third scenario involves a coastal migration using water craft along the edges of the ice sheets of the North Atlantic (Stanford and Bradley 2012). This "Solutrean Hypothesis" is based on the similarity of leaf-shaped stone points on both sides of the Atlantic although the evidence is far from conclusive. A fourth scenario elaborated by Steve and Kathleen Holen called the "Mammoth Steppe Hypothesis" suggests that a human population may have migrated from Asia prior to the last glacial maximum, before 20,000 years ago and then were cut off from Asia by the huge ice sheets that formed (Holen and Holen 2013). It is interesting that none of the four scenarios are mutually exclusive.

The oldest undisputed Amerindian population in North America is the Clovis culture which lasted a mere 300 years from about 11,200 – 10,900 BCE. It is named after a distinctive "fluted" projectile point found in Clovis, New Mexico in the 1930's in direct association with extinct megafauna. There a few sites in the Americas with artifacts and features that appear to pre-date Clovis (such as Meadowcroft and Cactus Hill in North America, and Monte Verde in Chili) but the evidence is still inconclusive. For more on Clovis hunting see Waguespack 2003.

Paleoindian populations in North America were once viewed as exclusively relying on big-game, many of which are now extinct, for their subsistence. Additional research has revealed that they likely were also generalized hunters and foragers who took advantage of a wide variety of smaller animals and plants found late Pleistocene environments including open the open grasslands and deciduous forests.

The extinction of many species of megafauna (such as mammoth, mastodon, camel, ground sloth and others) in North America coincides generally with the arrival of humans. Paul Martin proposed a scenario placing the extinction of the megafauna on a blitzkrieg-style expansion of the Clovis population across the continent (Martin 1975, Mosimann and Martin 1975, Waguespack 2007). Other scenarios may be equally valid and it is important to remember that the post-glacial environment was changing rapidly and a variety of ecological factors, including possibly disease, were likely contributors.

Toward the end of the Pleistocene bison populations increased dramatically. Bison are herd animals and tend to stampede when frightened. There are numerous examples of spectacular communal kills, such as the Olsen-Chubbuck site in eastern Colorado and the Head-Smashed-In buffalo jump in Canada, where entire herds were stampeded into arroyos or off cliffs and killed. At the Olson-Chubbuck site it is estimated that only 16 percent of the nearly 200 bison killed were only partially butchered. This "gourmet butchering" was common and many dead animals show no signs of butchering.

Later Paleoindian populations include Folsom, Plainview, Goshen, Agate Basin, Hell Gap, and Alberta/Cody. These have been identified primarily by their distinctive spear stone points.

Archaic Period

The end of the Paleoindian period and the beginning of the Archaic period varies regionally in North America and each geographic region had its own particulars. There is an almost bewildering array of microenvironments but for general purposes the Archaic is defined by a shift from big game hunting and foraging to a more broad-spectrum hunting and gathering tradition. We see smaller projectile points and the appearance of grinding stones to process vegetable foods. In some regions of arctic North America the Archaic tradition for all practical purposes continues today.

As big game became scarce (everywhere except the bison on the Great Plains) many hunting groups relied more heavily on smaller animals such as deer, rabbits, turkey, and squirrels. Evidence suggests that they also relied more heavily on gathering vegetable foods, combined with fishing when possible. At sites like Danger Cave in Utah they were making nets, mats and baskets, and rope out of plant fibers.

In the Paleolithic period we envision small groups of people traveling widely over the landscape, perhaps gathering yearly at key locations (such as Lindenmeier in Colorado) to renew acquaintance, exchange goods, and acquire mates. Towards the end of the Paleolithic they had begun to "settle in". In the Archaic period populations increased, mobility was reduced, and we see evidence of base camps and seasonal rounds (transhumance) where groups took advantage of different microenvironments within a more limited geographic region at different times of the year but generally return to a base location for the summer months, particularly in riverine or lake areas.

The increase in sedentism at the end of the Archaic period corresponds with new storage technologies for nuts and possibly the invention of pemmican, which is a mix of dried meat, berries, and fat. During various times of the Archaic period we see pit houses as seasonal domestic residences in some regions.

The Koster site in Illinois provides a glimpse of human activity at one river valley location beginning about 7500 BCE until about AD 1200. The first visitors were Paleoindian, followed by early, middle, and late Archaic occupations. By the middle Archaic there is evidence of occupation during most of the year. We also see broad spectrum flora and fauna utilization, storage pits for nuts, and human burials. Some of the earliest dog burials North America are found here.

By the end of the Archaic there is evidence of increased trade and the first appearance of prestige goods, such as copper and seashells in some regions. We also see increased sedentism, social complexity, the appearance of elites, warfare, and the beginnings of agriculture.

Post-Archaic

The most important agricultural domesticates were maize, beans, and squash although maize was introduced from Mesoamerica relatively recently. Tobacco, gourds, and cotton are also key domesticates.

In eastern North America we see cultivation of native plants at about 2000 BCE although maize and bean agriculture did not arrive from the Southwest until about 1000 BCE (it was first introduced in the Southwest from Mesoamerica about a thousand years earlier). After 1000 BCE we see a series of chiefdoms in the Southeast and Midwest with burial mounds and elaborate earthworks. The earliest earthworks are attributed to the Poverty Point Culture in Southeast North America between 2200 BCE and 600 BCE.

The Adena tradition appeared about 700 BCE. This was an Early Woodland culture that occupied the Ohio valley and neighboring regions. The Hopewell is another Woodland mound builder culture that first appeared about AD 1. They were agriculturalists who also hunted and fished largely in the Ohio valley (Buikstra 1999).

By about AD 800 we see the appearance of the Mississippian people in the Mississippi valley and also portions of the Southeast. This tradition survived until European contact. Besides maize agriculture the Mississippian tradition is associated with warfare and powerful leaders and sometimes very large settlements such as Cahokia in Missouri with over 100 mounds and at one point was surrounded by wooded fortifications. The largest mound is the pyramid-like Monks Mound also the largest prehistoric mound structure in North America. This village dates to about AD 1050 and was in decline by about AD 1150 (Iseminger 2010, Mink 1992, Young et al. 2000).

Early farmers in the Southwest include the Mogollon culture, which likely emerged from Archaic roots at about 300 BCE and they disappeared from the archaeological record about AD 1150. The Mogollon are found in New Mexico and Arizona and they made use of an agricultural tradition along the rivers that also included hunting and gathering in the highlands. Later we find the Hohokam in Southern Arizona. These people raised maize, beans, cucurbits, and cotton and employed sophisticated irrigation techniques. We find Hohokam settlements all over the Southwest and in northern Mexico from AD 1100 to 1450. They also relied on gathering wild crops (Adler 2002, Rice and Redman 1993).

The Anasazi or Ancestral Pueblo tradition dates from about AD 1 to AD 1300 and is found in the Four Corners area of Utah, Arizona, Colorado and New Mexico. This includes the Mimbres culture (which is famous for their elaborately decorated ceramic bowls). The Ancestral Puebloan's are likely ancestral to the modern Pueblo Indians including the Hopi and Zuni. Corn was introduced to the region at about AD 400 and most of the agriculture occurred along riverbanks that periodically flooded and provided moisture to the flood area although they also utilized irrigation agriculture occasionally. There are at least six phases of this culture ranging from early Basketmaker to Late Puebloan. We also see the appearance of subterranean kivas at about AD 800 which were likely adaptations of earlier pit-houses, although the kiva is largely a ceremonial structure. Above-ground housing in structures called room blocks or Pueblos are also often associated with the ceremonial kivas (Snead 2002).

The Chaco Phenomenon dates to about AD 1050 when about 5,500 people lived in Chaco Canyon, New Mexico, although Chaco Canyon's earliest villages date to about AD 490. We see a series of "great houses" such as Pueblo Bonito at the junctions of major drainages. Pueblo Bonito is built in a "D" shape with room blocks that surround central courts and kivas. The dating for Southwest settlements is highly accurate because of the well-preserved wood beams that can be accurately dated to the year of construction based on the region's dendrochronological sequence (tree rings).

Pueblo Bonito alone may have housed up to 1,000 people. Another aspect of the Chaco Phenomenon is a series of straight "roads" that measure up to 40 feet wide and extend for up to 60 miles without veering direction regardless of the hills and deep gullies. It is thought that these "roads" were ceremonial rather than economic although evidence suggests an extensive trade network throughout the region, extending even into Mesoamerica for exotic bird feathers and chocolate (Bawaya 2014, Van Dyke 2004).

Another famous location dating to this period is Mesa Verde which dates to about AD 1130. We know that a great drought had begun in AD 1130 and lasted for half a century. Defensive structures were built in key locations during this period. By AD 1299 the settlements had been abandoned and the populations disbursed into neighboring regions, including most likely the Rio Grande valley where many Native American Pueblo people are found today. It is important to note that recent studies indicate that some of population of the Mesa Verde region probably could have sustained itself through the drought, and there were likely other factors involved in the abandonment and exodus.

Pacific Northwest Coast

By the time sea levels reached stable levels at about 6500 BCE the inhabitants of the Pacific Northwest had developed a sustainable maritime economy, thanks largely to the Japanese Current and the year-round predictability of abundant maritime resources. These were sedentary hunter-gatherers who did not engage in agriculture yet who developed elite social status by about 4000 BCE and engaged in inter-group warfare by about 2500 BCE. They made use of abundant cedar trees that grew along the coast for their canoes, longhouses, and totem-poles. The potlatch involving feasting and the redistribution of material goods was developed here.

Arctic

The Inuit and Aleut are two distinct hunter-gatherer cultural groups native to the Arctic and date from about 7000 BCE into modern times. They are the most Asian in terms of morphology of all indigenous Americans. They developed specialized adaptations in the coastal regions and in the interior. They are also likely the first Native Americans to come into contact with the Norse (in Newfoundland at about AD 1000 (at L'Anse aux Meadows). The Aleuts occupied the Aleutian Islands and portions of the mainland cost and took advantage of a maritime environment. The Inuit (and the Eskimo) are largely nomadic hunters whose territory extends from the Alaskan interior as far east as Greenland. They are descendants of the Thule tradition who were whale hunters and who developed the kayak.

Summary

Clearly the prehistory of North America is much more complex than can be presented in just a few pages. Since the first arrival of humans in North America we see regional diversification and specialization, we see the development large and complex sedentary agricultural societies, and perhaps even archaic states. But we also see a continuation of the hunter-gatherer lifestyle. After the arrival of the Europeans in the Caribbean and the introduction of new diseases there was a massive population decline. The introduction of the horse in the mid-16th century provided new opportunities for previously sedentary peoples to migrate to new areas and adopt new lifestyles. Today there are over 500 recognized Native American Tribes in North America and the story of each is unique and more varied in detail than I could possibly describe in this short book. For more on the region see Browman et al. 2013, and Milner and Wills, 2013. For more on Colorado which has everything from the Paleolithic to agriculture and perhaps early pre-states see Cassells 1997.

Table 10. Mesoamerica and the Caribbean
Unless otherwise stated dates are the beginning or earliest dates

Approx. Lakh Time	Key Event, Time Period, or Site	Approx. Date
11:59 PM	Today	
11:58 PM	Sputnik 1 Launched, Space Age Begins	1957
11:51 PM	Cortez Conquers Aztecs	1519
11:50 PM	Columbus Arrives in Bahamas	1492
11:45 PM	Aztecs Arrive in Valley of Mexico	1200
11:44 PM	Chichen Itza Largely Abandoned	1150
11:39 PM	Terminal Classic Period	800
11:38 PM	Teotihuacan Collapse	750
11:35 PM	Late Classic Period	600
11:34 PM	Teotihuacan at its Apex	500
11:33 PM	Copan Founded	435
11:33 PM	Palenque Founded	431
11:29 PM	Early Classic Period Begins	250
11:19 PM	City of Monte Alban Begins	400 BCE
11:19 PM	Late Preclassic Period Begins	400 BCE
11:17 PM	Saladoid Migration to Bahamas	500 BCE
11:14 PM	Taino Settle Bahamas	700 BCE
11:09 PM	Farming Communities in Lowlands Begin	1,000 BCE
11:05 PM	Olmec Culture and Architecture Begins	1,200 BCE
10:52 PM	Second Migration into Caribbean	2,000 BCE
10:52 PM	Pottery (in gourd-like styles)	2,000 BCE
10:52 PM	Early to Middle Preclassic Period Begins	2,000 BCE
10:52 PM	Archaic Period Ends	2,000 BCE
10:33 PM	Mesoamerican Calendar "Start Date"	3,113 BCE
10:19 PM	Earliest Occupants in Caribbean	4,000 BCE
10:14 PM	Earliest Maize Possibly Domesticated	4,300 BCE
9:12 PM	Bottle Gourds Possibly Domesticated	8,020 BCE
8:47 PM	Archaic Period Begins	9,500 BCE
8:05 PM	Paleoindian Period Generally Begins	12,000 BCE

16 MESOAMERICA AND THE CARIBBEAN

Regional Overview

The Mesoamerican region extends from the northern border of Mexico to the southern boundary of Panama, and for the purpose of this chapter will also include the Caribbean. To the north are the highlands and the Basin of Mexico, a little farther south is the Valley of Oaxaca. South of Oaxaca is the Yucatan lowland area and even farther south we find the tropical rainforests of the highlands in southern Mexico and Guatemala. The region is bordered on the east by the Gulf of Mexico and on the west by Sierra Madre mountain range and the Pacific Ocean. The relatively low-lying Yucatan has few rivers, shallow soils, and a high-water table percolating through porous limestone bedrock.

There were no large herd animals native to the region and no large navigable rivers although there was a large array of plant resources. The earliest cultigens were bottle gourd and squash dating to about 10,000 years ago. It is possible that these were prized as containers, more than as food, which raises interesting questions about the early purpose of agriculture in the region (more below). Maize cultivation apparently developed later, by about 6,300 years ago. Trade and cultural contact extended north into what is today the southwestern United States and south into Panama and Colombia. Mesoamerican crops were of a wide variety and included the bottle gourd, squash, beans, chili pepper, cocoa, vanilla, cotton, agave, grain amaranth, and maize, to name just a few.

Archaic Period

Nomadic bands of highly mobile, low-population, hunter-gatherers characterized the region during this time, likely descendent from their Paleolithic ancestors (discussed earlier). Some of the earliest experiments with plant domestication occurred during this period. For example, the earliest dated bottle gourd rind is 8020-7915 BCE. Gourd like fruits can be used as net floats, containers, and rattles. Recent DNA analysis of gourds in the Americas cluster them with Asian, rather than African subspecies, which suggests that the plant was introduced from Asia possibly during the late Pleistocene.

The earliest directly dated maize cobs date to approximately 4300 BCE and are quite small, possibly retaining some traits of wild teosinte, which is the most likely precursor. Evidence of even earlier possible maize cultivation on the Gulf coast dates to 5000 BCE. Beans may have also been domesticated at much the same time but the evidence is lacking. Seasonal slash and burn maize farming may have also have begun during this period.

Early to Middle Pre-Classic

This period is marked by the first introduction of pottery along the Pacific coast and then about a century later in the Tehuacan valley. The earliest pottery seems to mimic vessels made from gourds. The earliest sedentary communities in the region date to about 1600 BCE but did not yet appear to depend entirely on agriculture. Burnt remains of a possible timber palisade at San Jose Mogote indicate the possibility of raiding and warfare. Farming communities begin to appear in the tropical lowlands by about 1000 BCE.

The Olmec culture dates to approximately 1200 BCE to 400 BCE and is located on the coast and some inland areas along the southern edge of the Gulf of Mexico. Some have called the Olmec the "mother culture" of Mesoamerica but this remains controversial although here is little controversy that they contributed to the region's ideas, traditions, art, and religion. The Olmec are best known for the huge sculptures of stone heads. One of the earliest Olmec sites is San Lorenzo dating from about 1250 BCE to 900 BCE. This site included an earthen pyramid and possibly an elite residence. Large rubber balls were placed in a nearby spring-fed pond which suggests an origin to the ball game that is ubiquitous to the region.

While there are no known Olmec ball courts, some carved figures wear what appears to be ball game gear. The later Aztecs referred to the descendants of the Olmec as the "rubber people" because of the tribute they paid in rubber. The colossal carved stone heads at San Lorenzo were quarried from a rock source about 37 miles away. Some of these weigh more than 40 tons. La Venta, dating from about 800 BCE to 400 BCE, rose to significance after the decline of San Lorenzo and is notable for evidence of maize symbolism and for rich mortuary evidence from the graves of infants that suggest the emergence of inherited rank and social position. This may be evidence of an early state rather than chiefdom. The Olmec traded in jade, obsidian, rubber, and their pottery style is widespread over the region.

In western Mexico we see societies with a distinctive pottery style and a shaft-tomb burial tradition. Many sites lack monumental buildings although recent surveys suggest there may have been large population centers. There is argument that maritime contacts existed between portions of western Mexico and South America based on similarities of pottery style, dress, and metallurgy with parts of Ecuador. The pottery figurines include sculptures of houses, rituals, ball games, musical performances, and people being carried in litters (Beekman 2010).

Late Pre-Classic

This period is characterized by a changing settlement patterns and the rise of large political centers, actual cities, such as Monte Alban in the Valley of Oaxaca and Teotihuacan in the Valley of Mexico. We also see the origins of the Mesoamerica calendar, counting, and writing.

Jonathan Friedman's model (from another region) for the emergence of ranked societies (1979) has been sometimes applied to this period of Mesoamerica. According to Friedman "egalitarian" villages composed of lineages of equal prestige all trace their origin to a remote ancestor. In time, one lineage (by one method or another but Friedman suggests hard work) acquires enough resources to rise in stature. Public opinion then sees the success of the lineage as evidence that it has a stronger connection with the distant common ancestor and the leader eventually becomes a hereditary ruler who serves as a mediator between the community and the supernatural. (Note: a similar type of "circular reasoning" is used by some rulers today to justify their wealth, status, and special privileges.) This is slightly different that the militaristic state-emergence scenario proposed by Carnerio (1970) discussed earlier in "first to market" terms. Both warrant consideration.

Monte Alban, in the Valley of Oaxaca is one of the first great cities in Mesoamerica and dates from approximately 400 BCE to AD 700. At its peak this was a vast ceremonial center with pyramid-temples, public architecture, private housing zones, and perhaps hereditary elite. There are figures carved in stone of what may be dead and tortured enemies. Several other polities have been identified in the valley.

Teotihuacan, in the Basin of Mexico, was a dominant political and cultural center for all of Mesoamerica at its apex in approximately AD 500. The city was laid out on a north-south axis, centered on the Avenue of the Dead. It was comprised of plazas, markets, temples, palaces, outlying apartment buildings, and complex drainage systems. It was dominated by the Pyramid of the Sun and the Pyramid of the Moon. There is evidence of foreign quarters which may have housed visitors or even hostages, from other regions. Human sacrifice became increasingly prominent in later centuries. The city may have housed up to 120,000 people, compared to 60,000 for Montel Alban.

The city collapsed as the major political power around AD 700 to AD 750. perhaps because of internal fractional conflict. This is theorized because there simply were no other major power sources in the region that were strong enough to be a viable threat. There is evidence of burning and deliberate destruction of major temples and tombs. By the sixteenth century the city had a population of perhaps 10,000, a mere fraction of its former glory. The rise, fluorescence, and fall of Teotihuacan is a consistent pattern characteristic of Mesoamerican civilization (Blanton et al. 1996, Fox 1996).

Mesoamerican Counting and Calendar

The Mesoamerican numerical, writing and calendar systems probably had their origins with the Olmec, although they reached their apex with the Maya. While our contemporary counting system is a decimal or base-10 system, with one number for each finger on both hands, the Mesoamerican counting system was a base-20 system. Numbers are noted with dots (for one) and bars (for five). The Mesoamerican calendar tracks cycles of 260 days and 365 days.

The 260-day calendar (called the *tzolkin* cycle) is unique in the world and does not appear to correspond to anything in particular. It may be a permutation of the number 20; it appears to correspond with the human gestation period between birth and conception which is Approximately 266 days. Some think it could be connected with the 260-day average interval of the planet Venus's appearance as the morning star, and Venus is an important celestial figure in Mesoamerica and parts of North America.

A zero symbol was generally depicted as a seashell, or a closed fist, perhaps symbolizing completion. The 365-day count was referred to as the *haab*. Together these calendars constitute a 52-year Calendar Round, where each day has a unique *tzolkin* and *haab* name (and glyph or image). At the end of each 52-year cycle, a new cycle begins and therefore each day in all of Mesoamerican time has a unique name.

A third calendar, the Long Count, is a linear count of time. It began on August 11 in 3113 or 3114 BCE (depending on whether you count the year zero). In this system a day is a *kin*, a 20 day period is a *uinal*, a 360 day period is a *tun*, a 7,200 day period is a *k'atun*, and a 144,000 day period is a *baktun*. Note the progression of units is always by a factor of 20 except for the *tun*, which is 2 x18. This may have been a solar year accommodation to the counting system because 360 is closer to a solar year of 365 days than is 400 (20 x 20). In AD 2012 the Long Count tally of 1,872,000 days reverted to zero and a new Long Count period began (but nobody is counting this way now so does it matter?). Think of the odometer in your car, when it switches over to 000,0000 the engine does not explode, the odometer just starts counting again (Aveni 2009).

No one knows why the Long Count began when it did. It is suggested by some that that Maya astronomers essentially back-calculated to a mathematically significant date. Of note is the fact that the Long Count is made of 13 *baktuns* and both August 11, 3114 BCE and December 21, 2012 correspond to important positions of the solar cycle (solar zenith and solar standstill, or what we call today the winter solstice). Another explanation is that the date was chosen as a fabrication of a royal dynastic narrative covering such a vast period of time that its origin could not be challenged. Archaeologists can convert any Mesoamerican calendar date to a Gregorian calendar date thanks largely to some sixteenth-century documents from the Yucatan that identify dates on both calendars but the true origins of the Maya calendar remain elusive. Remember, Ussher theorized a start date of 4004 BCE using much less precise information (see above) but let us not overlap calendars or cultures in our regional quest.

Early Classic

The Classic period is broken into three sub-periods (archaeologists usually do that), Early, Late, and Terminal Classic. During this phase, which includes its fluorescence, the Maya civilization was far from uniform but it had the key characteristics of a 'Great Tradition' with its own architectural, religious, and artistic similarities. Fagan and Duranni put it well: "The Maya rulers were likely shaman-lords in the early stages (and divine) warrior-priest-kings in later times" (2014).

They seemingly prized social status above almost everything else. Kingship was usually passed from father to son, or brother to brother, in a line that lead back to the founding ancestor. Status was inherited and was the key way the legitimacy of society was maintained. Human sacrifice, mythical creatures, conquests, and dynastic histories make up a large amount of the Maya imagery. Religion seems to have unified the Maya more than other interests (Webster 2002).

In this period there were dozens of small polities and no regional capitols or well-defined settlement hierarchies. It appears that most wars were between immediate neighbors, and the capture and sacrifice of a ruler and prisoners of war was a method of validating political (and ancestral) authority. Most ceremonial centers were essentially autonomous, with agricultural activities dotting the landscape in-between. The first glyphs of named leaders (and their ancestry and activities) occur late in this period. It is widely thought that Teotihuacan may have had a direct influence in some early Maya political developments.

The western lowland (Yucatan) city of Palenque dates to this period. The dynastic history began on March 11 AD 431 when Jaguar-Quetzal became the ruler. As a descendent of a revered ancestor Pacal, he inherited the throne through his mother and reigned for 67 years. His tomb (found at the base of a pyramid, which is unusual) records a dynastic record legitimizing his reign that is present in later Maya religious imagery. The city of Palenque was a major power in the southwestern lowlands at the end of the Early Classic period. The tomb covering of Jaguar-Quetzal (showing him ascending to the heavens) is an iconic heritage reference in much of Central America today.

Late Classic

In the Late Classic period at least four major city-states reach regional dominance. Copan, Tikal, Caracal, and Palenque can be thought of as regional capitals ruling over a well-defined hierarchy of lesser settlements and hamlets with terraced fields and water reservoirs. During this period Maya civilization reached its peak in terms of population and complexity.

Tikal is in the southern lowland and actually is older than Palenque (discussed earlier). Tikal had its origins in the Late Preclassic. One later ruler (*ajaw*) was of Teotihuacan descent and a tradition of Teotihuacan influence flourished during his reign. Tikal's glyphs identify 31 rulers in a 669 year long succession, ending in AD 869,

Caracal, in south-central Belize and reached a population of more than 120,000 making it larger than Tikal to north. Records indicate that Caracal defeated Tikal in AD 562 and emerged as a major regional force.

Copan, in Honduras, is the southernmost of the four major city-states. The earliest inscription dates to December 11, AD 435. The city contains raised enclosed courtyards, pyramids, temples and plazas covering 30 acres. Clearly this was a time of conflict and consolidation, as we have seen in other regions of the world.

Terminal Classic/Early Postclassic/Conquest

Toward the end of the eighth century AD many of the great centers were abandoned, the Long Count calendar was discontinued, and the state structure was diminishing. The elite vanished and the population declined to about a third. The non-elite survivors clustered in the remnants of their residences and within a century even they too vanished from most of the area.

However, the Maya civilization did not vanish completely. New centers emerged in neighboring areas and the Maya civilization continued to flourish in the northern Yucatan at such places as Chichen Itza until long after the arrival of the Spaniards.

It is thought that a multiplicity of factors likely contributed to the earlier Maya collapse. The population had reached its peak, agricultural productivity fell (possibly due to soil depletion by growing maize and through a lack of other agricultural intensification strategies), and disease and malnutrition may have resulted.

Depletion of natural resources also likely occurred, particularly by cutting the rainforest for wood to not only cook with and build small structures, but also to heat lime to make plaster to cover the grand structures of the elite (Coulter 2009).

Mesoamerica may have reached and exceeded its carrying capacity and severe drought cycles during the end of the period may have tipped the scales against them. At this time the elite seem to have vanished. What good was a warrior-god-king and his court if there is no food to eat?

The period of Maya collapse caused vast population movements and saw the arrival in central Mexico of invaders from the northwest. One of these was the Toltec. They settled at Tula, south of the Valley of Mexico, and built a ceremonial center for their serpent god, Quetzalcoatl, who required only the sacrifice of butterflies (for more on the Maya see Browman et al. 2013, Clark and Blake, 1994, Demarest 1992, Webster 2013),

By the early postclassic the Toltec also interacted with the remaining Maya. Architectural evidence of this mixture is evident at Chichen Itza, which was largely but not completely abandoned at about AD 1150. One of the most famous structures at Chichen Itza is the central pyramid with the head of Kukulkahn (or feathered serpent in the Mayan language, otherwise known in the region as Quetzalcoatl). Warrior images celebrating conquest and human sacrifice are also present.

The Aztecs, like the Toltecs, may have migrated to the Valley of Mexico relatively early in twelfth century. "Aztec" is really a collective label for several groups including the Mexica, Acolhua, Tepaneca, and Chalca peoples. One group, the Mexica and settled onto the small islands of Lake Texcoco and built what was to become the Aztec capitol of Tenochtitlan which housed perhaps 200,000 people (it is today modern-day Mexico City). The modern nation of Mexico has its named origins in this scenario, like so many others mentioned earlier.

The Aztec empire was a mosaic of about 400 regional alliances fueled by an elaborate tribute-gathering system that ran for the benefit of the elite. One record indicates that 26 cities served to only provide firewood for one royal palace. The elite ruled through marriage alliances, taxation, and military conquest. Aztec religion also required the constant placation of the war and rain gods (Huitzilopochtli and Tlaloc) through human sacrifice and ritual cannibalism by the elites that may have been orchestrated to cement their status. The Aztecs were not well-liked by their subjects and there is evidence that the living standards for commoners declined under Aztec rule.

A formidable opponent of the Aztec were the Tarascans to the west. They occupied the region previously identified by the shaft-tomb tradition in the Early to Middle Preclassic. Another opponent was the Tlaxcalan confederation to the east.

In 1519 the Aztec empire may have reached its peak, or it may have had a long and prosperous (but characteristically violent) future ahead of it. Given Mesoamerican patterns it probably was destined for a relatively quick and unpleasant end (at least for the elites). All that changed on a propitious day in 1519 with the arrival of Hernan Cortez and about 500 men with armor and guns. They landed on the shores of the Aztec empire on the very day that prophesies said Quetzalcoatl (the benevolent hero-king of the Toltec) would return (we have seen this before in Oceania).

By 1520 the reigning emperor Moctezuma II was dead and in August of 1521 the great city of Tenochtitlan lay in ruins under Spanish dominion, and the elites were gone, thanks partly to alliances forged by Cortez with the several Aztec enemies. The remaining Aztec empire was destroyed by the Spaniards in about one year.

The Maya were initially spared by the Spaniards because they did not have the hordes of gold that the Aztecs had accumulated. The Spanish conquest of the remaining Maya began about twenty years later and the Maya actually held out in the dep forests of northern Guatemala until 1697 until they were overcome by the Spanish, ending a 4,000-year-old cultural 'Grand Tradition' (something similar happened with the Inca, see below).

The Caribbean

The Caribbean islands extend from the Bahamas off the coast of Florida to the Lesser Antilles off the Coast of Venezuela. The earliest traces of human occupation are in Cuba, the Dominican Republic, and Haiti. They date to about 4,000 BCE which is only a few centuries after maize was domesticated in Mesoamerica.

The first colonization in the Caribbean is likely to have originated from the southern Yucatan in Belize at about 4000 BCE, similar artifacts have been found in both areas. There is evidence that people arrived without planning because they had to adapt to the local flora and fauna and did not introduce new species. Over time various islands were colonized and this suggests a boat-building technology capable of traveling between islands.

A second migration into the region occurred about 2000 BCE and brought with them axes, bowls, ground stone and portable art, but no ceramics (pottery). This was a seafaring culture. A later migration, about 500 BCE is called the Saladoid migration brought pottery and permanent settlements. It seems that this migration may have been planned because they brought cultivated South American crops with them.

By AD 700 the Bahamas were settled under a group of chiefdoms called the Taino. Populations grew in most of the islands and village farmers first appear. Larger political entities appear in the larger islands and we see ceremonial plazas, ball courts (with perhaps a Mesoamerican connection), and ceremonial artifacts. They were based on the cultivation of the South American root crop manioc and by fishing. The Taino were also seafaring traders.

The Taino had large oceangoing canoes (some reportedly holding a hundred people) and were characterized by a dramatic cultural expansion as evidenced by ceremonialism, beadwork, ceramics, weaving and woodworking. This ended in 1492 with the arrival of Christopher Columbus. Disease apparently destroyed most of the Taino chiefdoms within a decade. Columbus later referred to them as the "Caribs". They were known as fierce fighters and possibly as cannibals. Their descendants are part of a rich multicultural heritage in a complex and little-understood archaeological region.

THE LONG WALK HERE

Table 11. South America – Andes and Amazon

Unless otherwise stated dates are the beginning or earliest dates

Approx. Lakh Time	Key Event, Time Period, or Site	Key Dates
11:59 PM	Today	
11:58 PM	Sputnik 1, Space Age Begins	1957
11:51 PM	Last Inca Emperor Executed	1572
11:51 PM	Pizzaro Conquers Inca	1530
11:50 PM	Inca Empire	1476
11:44 PM	Chimu Empire in N. (Chan Chan)	1100
11:42 PM	Late Intermediate Period	1000
11:40 PM	Sican State (North) and Sea Trade	900
11:36 PM	Middle Period	650
11:36 PM	Wari State	650
11:34 PM	River Based Amazon chiefdoms	500
11:29 PM	Tiwanaku State (South)	200
11:22 PM	Intermediate Period	200 BCE
11:22 PM	Moche State (North), Irrigation Ag	200 BCE
11:22 PM	Nasca (South)	200 BCE
11:05 PM	Chavin de Huantar	1,200 BCE
11:00 PM	Caral Abandoned	1,500 BCE
11:00 PM	Settled Villages (North Coast)	1,500 BCE
11:00 PM	Woven cotton, pottery	1,500 BCE
10:55 PM	Andes Initial Period	1,800 BCE
10:42 PM	Caral (City complex)	2,627 BCE
10:35 PM	Paleolithic Period Generally Ends	3,000 BCE
10:35 PM	Andes Preceramic Period	3,000 BCE
10:27 PM	Agriculture in Amazon	3,500 BCE
10:10 PM	Earliest Coastal Textiles	4,500 BCE
9:04 PM	Hunter-Gatherers in Amazon	8,500 BCE
8:05 PM	Paleolithic Period Generally Begins	12,000 BCE
7:28 PM	Monte Verde (possibly earlier)	14,220 BCE

17 SOUTH AMERICA – ANDES AND AMAZON

Regional Overview

This overview begins in the late Pleistocene and ends with the Spanish conquest of the Inca in AD 1533. The region extends along the west coast of South America from the northern border of Colombia south to Tierra del Fuego and includes some of the driest landscapes, some of the highest mountains, and some of the richest off-coast fisheries in the world. It boasts the world's longest river, longest mountain range, and largest tropical forest.

Few suitable animals were available for domestication but those that were include the llama, alpaca, and guinea pig. Cotton, peppers, beans, squash, peanuts, quinoa, manioc (a root plant also knows as cassava), and potatoes were the chief plant domesticates. Limited maize agriculture along the coast was introduced in approximately 2500 BCE.

The preindustrial states that developed in the region can be viewed from north-south mountain and coastal perspective. Cultural developments occurred relatively independently in the northern regions and in the southern regions. The two were united only recently under the Inca Empire.

Paleolithic

One of the oldest sites in the all the Americas is in southern Chile. This site, Monte Verde, has been radio-carbon dated to approximately 14,220 BCE, although a much older component may exist. The site is covered in a peat bog and the level of preservation is extraordinary for a site this old.

Monte Verde has not only stone artifacts but well-preserved bone and wooden materials. There are two rectangular "houses" that would likely have been skin-covered. Wooden tent stakes and a child's footprint have been uncovered beside a clay-lined hearth, with associated wooden mortars and vegetable foods. The occupants would have hunted small game and possibly camels and mastodons. Wood was apparently the most important raw material and was used for hafting stone tools; three such hafted stone scrapers have been uncovered. Wild vegetables that were exploited include potatoes the chewable bolo-plant (whose leaves are used today to make a type of medicinal tea).

Maritime Hypothesis

Unlike many civilizations around the world, the Andean civilization may not have had an agricultural foundation. Rather, the basis of subsistence may reside in the ecological differences between the arid coast and the rugged Andes, which are second only to the Himalayas in height. The key here is that one of the world's richest fishery lies off the Pacific shoreline. Anchovies are one of the primary fish relatively easily netted off the coast and today support millions of people.

Michael Moseley and his colleague Michael Heckenberger (2013) have analyzed the region and suggest that the maritime resources of the Pacific Coast provided sufficient calories to support sedentary populations that clustered in large communities near the coast. As populations rose this preadapted them to large-scale agriculture.

Small mesh nets and gourd floats have been recovered from several South American coastal sites, which support this. There is an argument that the maritime resources alone would have not supported large populations and that trade with the highland areas was necessary. In essence, a symbiotic relationship between the coast (with fish, salt, and iodine-rich seaweed) and the highlands (with gourds for nets, cotton for netting, potatoes, and other carbohydrate foods) would have been established. This hypothesis helps explain why coastal materials have been found in the highlands and visa versa. It also helps explain why states formed in both the lowlands and the highlands.

Andes Preceramic

Complex societies developed near the coast at least 5,000 years ago. This was a large area anchored by a center in the Supe Valley known as Caral, about twelve miles inland from the Pacific and about 120 miles north of

Lima, Peru. Many agricultural products including guavas, beans, peppers, fruit, cotton, and gourds were there. These items would have been traded with the coastal population for anchovies. Indeed, anchovies have been found in human feces from the site.

Caral is comprised of six large stone platforms made of quarried stone and filled with cobbles from the nearby Supe River. The cobbles were carried to the site and deposited in nets, which have been radiocarbon dated to approximately 2627 BCE. There are several sunken plazas, apartment complexes, modest houses, and grand residences suggesting a burgeoning class distinction.

Caral is considered by some to be a city (but maybe not occupied full time by everyone), and it was the largest settlement in the Americas a full 1,500 years before Teotihuacan in Mexico. In a sense it was all alone at the time. It dates to the time of the earliest Egyptian pharaohs and is the earliest preindustrial semi-state in the Americas.

For unknown reasons it was abandoned between 2000 and 1500 BCE. Interestingly, there is no pottery associated with the agricultural activity at Caral but there is evidence of the use of hallucinogenic substances possibly associated with ceremony and ritual. Maize beer would not appear until just before the Initial Period along the coast.

Andes Initial Period

We see sedentary villages appearing in the lowlands of the north coast between 2500 and 1800 BCE. This period saw the development of highland societies. There is also evidence of cotton weaving and the later development of very fine textiles made of cotton and wool at this time. After about 1800 BCE we see a set of interacting chiefdoms emerge along the northern and central parts of the coast. Pottery first appears in the archeological record during this time, long after the demise of Caral.

There is a growing use of massive ceremonial buildings, including a distinctive U-shaped platform and widespread use of common art motifs during the Initial Period (particularly on the coast). Ceremonial complexes were covered with clay (not plaster as we saw in Mesoamerica) and were brightly painted. There are few signs of burial rituals suggesting social ranking or personal wealth, although some type of leadership would have been required for the massive construction projects. We also see the beginnings of irrigation agriculture during this sequence.

Some of the artwork depicts armed men with dismembered human remains suggesting conflict and warfare. During this period the site of Chavin de Huantar was constructed, perhaps by 1200 BCE. The ceremonial center features a large ceremonial pyramid with u-shaped plaza and a sunken courtyard. The art styles and motifs found here may represent a "mother culture" for later Andean civilizations. Interestingly, these are forest animals and may suggest early contact with the Amazonian interior.

Much of what we know about early textiles comes from the mummies of the Paracas Peninsula along the coast and from the Chinchorro culture of this period. They were usually found in a fetal position and were wrapped in brightly colored cotton and/or wool blankets. Many of these mummy bundles were placed in small chambers or stone-lined subterranean vaults with wooden roofs where the dry conditions provided for their excellent preservation.

Other developments during this period include the rise of complexity in the highlands as evidenced by the Chiripa on the shore of Lake Titicaca and later by the Pukara at about 400 BCE. (located about 47 miles northwest of Lake Titicaca). Based on the architectural and stylistic evidence these may have been ancestral to the later site of Tiwanaku.

Andes Early Intermediate Period

This period is known for the Moche state on the northern coast and the Nasca region in the south. In the north we see large ceremonial centers with finely finished administrative and residential quarters and humbler dwellings on the outskirts. The soils were planted with simple wooden digging sticks, just as they are today, but agricultural intensification and associated bureaucratic controls were also in place. These include irrigation agriculture (and strict water flow controls) along with terracing.

The Moche state flourished for approximately 800 years, beginning in about 200 BCE, with great ceremonial centers and huge irrigation works. It was a multi-valley state that may have comprised several satellite centers that ruled over individual valleys. To say that Moche pottery is finely modeled is an understatement. Moche pottery was exquisite in its representational detail of individuals and daily life.

Many of the human burials are well-preserved in the dry desert sand and these provide a wealth of information about Moche society. One such spectacular burial, at Sipan, held the body of a warrior-priest in his full regalia, including a gold mask, llamas, and several adults, two were perhaps part of the lord's entourage.

Moche art depicts warrior-priests wearing a crescent-shaped headdress on a conical helmet, very much like the regalia found in earlier tombs. We do not know exactly how Moche society was organized but it appears that a ruler wielded authority over a hierarchical state of warrior-priests, specialists, and the mass of the agricultural population. The elite likely used tax labor to build their huge temples. This is a technique that later states and empires would utilize.

A series of natural disasters struck the Moche in the late sixth century AD. The first may have been a drought lasting approximately 30 years that ended in AD 594. El Nino events may have brought torrential rains that washed away entire irrigation systems, one such event likely flooded the imperial capital just before AD 600. Sometime between AD 650 and 700 a large earthquake struck and the landslides apparently choked entire rivers with debris and silt.

During this period, we also see the Nazca (to the south) who are best known for the "geoglyphs" of the Nazca plains. These are lines and figures that were created by removing the upper dark rocks and sediments to expose lower, lighter-colored surfaces. Sizable areas can be cleared with relatively little work. There are more than 300 geometric figures and over 620 miles of straight lines on the plains. They may have been constructed to be walked on, rather than to be viewed. The Nazca people were weavers and potters who lived in simple farming communities. A central Nazca ceremonial place, Cahuachi, has more than 40 modest sized mounds and a Great Temple.

Andes Middle Horizon

This period is a turning point in Andean prehistory and is characterized by the Tiwanaku and Wari empires in the central and in the southern highlands.

The Tiwanaku state dates to approximately AD 200 and was located in the high, flat country surrounding Lake Titicaca. The population apparently raised enormous herds of llama. They also practiced agriculture based on a raised-field system surrounded with irrigation canals. The water in the canals maintained warmth at night and may have provided protection for potatoes and other plants against harsh frosts. The fields were highly fertile; the soils were enriched by decaying plant materials and fish from the surrounding canals. In recent years, archaeologists have worked with local villages to reintroduce this ancient agricultural technology.

The Wari state dates to approximately AD 600 and was the site of a highland urban and ceremonial center with huge stone walls and associated dwellings that cover several square miles. The Wari domain extended from Moche country in the north into the highlands south of Cuzco. The Wari art style shows some influence from the earlier Pukara (a state northwest of Lake Titicaca dating to about 400 BCE), including anthropomorphic feline, eagle, and serpent beings. Wari expansion was probably achieved through conquest, trade, and religious means. The Wari elite controlled food supplies and labor and built storehouses for food and roads reminiscent of the later Inca.

For unknown reasons both the Tiwanaku and Wari domains collapsed at the end of the first millennium.

Andes Late Intermediate Period

This is not a simple transition sequence. The earlier decline of the Moche left somewhat of a vacuum filled by the Sican domain in the North that was later overthrown by the Chimu, who were in tern were dominated by the Inca.

The Sican domain lasted a scant 200 years from about AD 900 to 1100. The burial of a Sican lord in the La Leche Valley revealed much about the society. The lord was dressed in full regalia (with sacrificial victims) and elaborate ornaments in gold, gold and silver alloy, and bronze. The Sican also apparently engaged in seagoing trade in copper and other materials as far north as Ecuador. After disruptive floods that were likely caused by another El Nino event, Sican was overthrown and burned by the expanding Chimu state which created the first regional empire.

Chimu controlled more than 12 river valleys through an extensive irrigation and administrative system. They built large water storage reservoirs and terraced hundreds of miles of steep hillsides. They built water channels that provided water even in periods of extreme drought; one canal extended nearly 20 miles to the Chimu capital, Chan Chan.

Chan Chan was a huge complex of walled compounds near the Pacific at the mouth of the Moche Valley. It covers nearly four square miles and consists of nine large walled enclosures. The walls were likely not built for defensive purposes but to provide physical and ritual isolation.

The Chimu domain was apparently a hierarchical society with strict social classes. Local leaders ruled various provinces. Tribute and labor likely were paid to the rulers by the commoners who worked on the irrigation system and in military service. A vast network of roadways connected each valley with the capitol and was used for trade and military action. When a new area was conquered the inhabitants were apparently resettled in a previously placated area and assimilated into the larger empire. This practice was also later adopted by the Inca.

The vast network of water storage and irrigation systems that characterized the Chimu Empire may also have contributed to its demise. The reservoirs could only last one or two lean seasons and the soils of the terraced hillsides may have become to saline for agriculture so food production dropped just when the population was reaching its peak. This delicate balance may have left the empire vulnerable to military conquest from outside. This may be just what happened when the Inca conquered them in the late 1460s.

Andes Late Horizon

This period is characterized by the Inca, who are relative latecomers in the archaeology of the Andes and who carried on many of the traditions of their predecessors. Inca can refer to both the ruler and the people. The Inca probably began as a petty chiefdom that was part of a military confederacy of groups in the southern highlands. A leader named Viracocha Inca rose to power at the beginning of the fifteenth century and became a living god in the first of a short series of hereditary rulers.

The Inca was a hierarchical, militaristic, autocratic society. The state was supported by the labor of the adult males who worked two or three months each year to maintain the vast infrastructure of roads, bridges, canals, agricultural terraces, serve in the military, and carry out state building projects (an effective tax rate of about 25% when you think about it) (MacQuarrie 2007).

The Inca Empire was centered in Cuzco and divided into four large provinces, each subdivided into smaller provinces. The empire was known as Tawantinsuyu or "The Land of the Four Quarters". Each new ruler had prestige but no possessions. The new Inca ruler had to acquire wealth and the mantle of leadership through military conquest. The Inca army was powerful and the only way a new ruler could obtain his own royal estate was by expansion into new territory and to provide ongoing labor-tax, thus this system of expansion had to be permanent. In this way the Inca Empire was destined to be an ever-expanding one, or to fail.

Part of the Inca control over the vast empire was based on a system of secondary non-Inca nobility who governed a taxpaying subpopulation. It also depended on an efficient road system for communication, trade, and military mobility. Inca records were kept on knotted strings, called *quipu*. Although the Spanish observed the *quipu* recordkeeping system they did not record how it was done. Efforts to decipher the *quipu* are ongoing.

The Inca Empire was overthrown by a small group of Spaniards led by Francisco Pizarro (a distant cousin of Hernan Cortez) in 1533 with the execution of the Inca emperor Atahualpa. A small group of rebel fighters led largely by one of Atahualpa's younger brothers held out for several decades in a jungle fortress on the Amazon side of the Andes (known as Vilcabamba) but they were ultimately silenced with the execution of the last Inca emperor, Tupac Amaru, in 1572.

Contrary to popular belief the famous tourism site of Machu Picchu was not an Inca rebel fortress but a summer palace for the Inca nobility. When Hiram Bingham (famous archaeologist and later a politician) "discovered it" in 1911 it was actually occupied by a few farming families that he quickly displaced with a few American dollars.

Amazonia

Amazonia is the largest ecological zone in South America and probably the least understood archaeologically. The earliest inhabitants date to about 8500 BCE and were hunter-gatherers. There is evidence of early agriculture by about 3500 BCE. The region likely supported numerous powerful chiefdoms and perhaps larger social endeavors.

The Saladoid peoples of the Orinoco River in northern Venezuela (who later spread north into the Caribbean) lived in villages whose huts surrounded a central plaza. The Arawak and Tupi-Guarani people occupied the Amazon lowlands to the south and were organized in small chiefdoms with large fortified villages. Aerial surveys suggest a complex human-modified landscape of enclosures, roads, and small oval mounds may lie beneath the jungle canopy.

By AD 500 to 1,000 local chiefdoms with dense populations were well established along the major Amazonian rivers. They interacted regularly and the standardized polychrome pottery suggest much cultural homogeneity over the region.

The Marajo site in the Amazon estuary dates from about AD 400. Here it is apparent that artificial mounds served as ceremonial structures and also as cemeteries. The dead were placed in special burial urns. There is evidence of an elite class. Upstream the Santarem culture constructed a dense settlement over an area of about ten square miles. The Santarem culture survived into historical times.

The people of the upper Amazon had a complicated relationship with the polities of the Andes, including trade. The last stronghold of the Inca (Vilcabamba) was located in upper Amazonia and it is clear in the archaeological record that the two spheres interacted.

In central Amazonia, the Acutuba settlement is known for its huge sunken amphitheaters and nearby settlements. Southern Amazonia was a densely populated series of chiefdoms, many with carefully planned plaza villages. Agricultural production included manioc cultivation, intensive fishing, and fruits.

Recent research suggests that the Pre-Columbian (before Columbus) population of the Amazon region may have been much larger than we thought. New aerial reconnaissance techniques are expanding our understanding of this region and new information is transforming our knowledge almost daily.

18 CONCLUSION

Clearly, humans are adaptive creatures.

The archaeological record demonstrates that we go long periods without changing much and we change a lot in relatively short periods, both physically and socially, but our social capabilities, generally summed up as culture, are key to our success. We also tend to vastly underestimate our ancestors' abilities. They did a lot more with much less than we have at our disposal today.

I don't know what any individual human will do in the future but I can largely guarantee to you they will align with groups and these groups will affiliate with (or fight) other groups and these alliances (and truces) will change over time. They will symbolically differentiate themselves within and between their groups because they are symbolic creatures.

So, what have we learned? Are we creatures of our ancient genetic heritage living under our clothes as "naked apes"? Are we creatures of our modern society? Yes to both. Our destiny seems to be to simultaneously live in two worlds, biological and cultural. This is not a new revelation to anyone, particularly philosophers or parents, but it is a good thing to keep in mind as we go about our daily modern business, like walking (bipedalism) while texting (socializing) … a dangerous combination for many.

So why does it all matter? From the physical evidence that is archaeology, it seems that it matters because as we create our future we desperately want to anchor it in our perceived past. Archaeology helps shed a new light on that past based on the material evidence.

I also think that we can better structure our social institutions and make more informed policy decisions when our citizens and leaders have a more complete understanding of the "patterns of prehistory". For example, there has been much in the popular media about the pace of change in the past few decades, but by putting this into perspective we realize that things really began changing relatively fast with the adoption of agriculture and settled communities millennia ago, long before our industrial and digital transitions.

With the understanding of the timeline of prehistory and the study of the rise and fall of societies large and small, we can see how fleeting individual lives are and how fragile our social institutions are. We can cherish and protect them or we can do the opposite. It is our choice.

As my beginning quote from Kierkegaard said: *Life can only be understood backwards; but it must be lived forwards.*

So, let us close this book (after reading Chapter 20), and continue our long 3.6 million-year walk and see if we really do learn anything from the past.

19 POSTSCRIPT

This chapter includes some "food for thought" on various topics in no particular order that I have occasionally used as discussion fodder in a classroom setting. Most, but not all, of the items relate to hunter-gatherers and provide a slightly different perspective on many things we do as we live our daily lives.

Is There is a Little Hunter-Gatherer in All of Us?

Consider for a moment that 95%-99% of the time people lived on this planet they were hunter-gatherers. In a way the up-side of the hunter-gatherer lifestyle (but do not forget there is also a downside) is like the idyllic lifestyle where you get to travel, try new foods, you don't have to work much (just shop), and you can spend time socializing. Who doesn't like to go shopping and bring home a bag of goodies for everyone in the family, who wouldn't love to work 20 hours a week doing a variety of things to bring home the food, (it has been said that "if work is so great how come more rich people don't do it?"), who usually fails to plan well for the future but instead considers immediate needs, who doesn't generally hate to follow instructions or leaders, and the list goes on. Note, I am not suggesting we all become hunter-gatherers tomorrow, I am just making an observation.

This is a bit of an evolutionary anthropology perspective because it presumes that much of our behavior is determined by genetics. We know that there is no "hunter-gatherer" gene and that hunter-gatherers invented sedentary-farming (the reasons why are unclear but many think it was more of an adaptation to changing environments and perhaps population pressure than an invention). Nonetheless, the little notion of "what if" there really is a bit of a genetic twist or flavor that we carry with us from our ancestral past that actually does affect our behavior. This is an area of biological anthropology and of cognitive archaeology that promises to be very interesting as we learn more about our neurology and how our behavior is affected by both nature and nurture.

Storage

Boxes, closets, attics, basements, garages, and storage units. When you think about it we collect and organize, label, and store all kinds of stuff. Hunter-gatherers generally had no storage because, by definition (generally), they were on the move and lots of stuff just slowed them down. In contrast, sedentary agriculturalists (also by definition) rely on storage of grain and other harvested food for future use.

The late George Carlin had a skit on "On Stuff" that is available on YouTube (posted in 2007 with over 6.9 million views) that makes this point very clear in a humorous fashion. The world of hunter-gatherers was a minimalist one, with "limited wants and unlimited means" (Gowdy 1998) that relied basically on an immediate return on labor. Sure, some short-term storage was possible (in pits, trees, and hanging from poles), as was the long-term caching of materials for future use when they returned to the same location. The difference between having stuff and not having stuff leads to some pretty profound thought experiments concerning the concept of ownership, possessions, redistribution, sharing, and even taxation.

Leaders, Taxes, and Slavery

Hunter-gatherers typically do not have formal, permanent, or hereditary leaders. Their leadership is 'just in time' for the hunt or expedition or feast, for example. It is a merit-based system of leadership where the best available person for the job is selected and who leads by influence not so much by fiat. Of course there are many variations to this but one thing they do not have, that sedentary agriculturists have, is taxes. There is nothing to tax. We see taxation in early civilizations where the leader appropriates a portion of the grain harvested by the population or requires eligible citizens to contribute their labor for special projects such as building or cleaning irrigation canals or building public structures. The Inca, for example, reportedly required about three months' work from the male head of household annually. Simple math suggests that their effective tax rate then was 25% (MacQuarrie 2007:158), which is less than most modern workers pay when you add up local, state, and federal taxes plus retirement contributions. For more on chiefs and leaders see Yoffee (1993).

Hunter-gatherers are known to take captives from other hunter-gatherer groups. Often these are women of breeding age and young children. In some cases there are methods for them to eventually integrate into the new group. Complex states also take captives, often through warfare, and they seem to have usually lived harsh lives as forced laborers. There is little about them in the early written record, but archaeologists are increasingly interested in learning more about this silent population. In his book *Against the Grain*, James Scott provides a thoughtful consideration of this element of early statehood (Scott 2017) and McGuire (1996).

Religion

In a remarkable book *Fields of Blood. Religion and the History of Violence* (2014) Karen Armstrong makes a strong case that organized religion gets blamed for many violent events in the past that could be more accurately ascribed to materialistic motives associated with territorial expansion, political control, and economic interests. She argues that the rationale or "excuse" for the conflicts were often couched in religious terms but the core motivation was often more secular. Although this is essentially a 'materialist' perspective, she also carefully and respectfully characterizes many of the core elements of the world's great religions

This raises some interesting questions concerning religion and the relationship between people and their god, or gods, or their concept of a supreme being, or the supernatural in general, or maybe nothing (it seems almost inescapable that everyone believes in something). Religion is so fundamental to the human experience that to ignore it, as many modern secular individuals are tempted to do, is like turning a blind eye to a big part of what it is to be human. Many of the earliest examples of modern human behavior have to do with the appearance of art and symbolism in the archaeological record at about 75,000 to 100,000 years ago. While this is not direct evidence of religious behavior, there is nothing to suggest that it isn't. Is the absence of evidence of something evidence of its absence?

Before the advent of science and the age of reason, religious traditions and sacred texts and stories were often the only way that humans had to make sense of their place in the world. Religious symbols are some of the most powerful symbols in the world and religious activity, particularly since the advent of sedentary agriculturalism, is an important part of the archaeological record. I tell my students that anyone who ignores religion in their study of humanity does so at their own peril. I am not advocating one religious perspective over another or criticizing the secular view, I am suggesting that archaeologists need to try to understand the importance of religion in prehistory.

Fermentation

In the right conditions fruits, grains, and even honey can ferment and produce an alcoholic substance. In some cases, it seems that the wild versions of these and similar items may have been valued and used not so much for food, but for their intoxicating effect. It helps to have pottery vessels available, but liquid can be held in watertight skin, animal stomachs, and even specially treated baskets. It is important to remember that our hunter-gatherer and early agricultural ancestors had a sophisticated knowledge of a wide variety of plant and animal resources available to them. To presume that all activities in prehistory are subsistence-based is to vastly narrow the scope of human behavior available for investigation and analysis (Smalley and Blake 2003).

Personality and Co-Dependency

We established earlier that humans are social creatures. Many creatures are social, including ants and bees and chimpanzees, but humans seem to have taken it to a new level, we are ultra-social. Hunter-gatherers typically live in small closely-related groups and they depend upon each other for survival in ways that 'independent' modern humans can barely comprehend. They know each other by sight, smell, sound, and touch. It has been said that by the standards of modern psychiatry they might be diagnosed as co-dependent personalities. I have discussed this with colleagues in psychiatry and they are quick to point out that the American Psychiatric Association's *Diagnostic and Statistical Manual of Mental Disorders is* a guideline that is meant to be taken in context and so a general diagnosis of a group would not be good practice. Nonetheless, it is food for thought. Let us also remember that the concept of personality dates only to the early 20th century and there have been different ways for people to explain individual dispositions and actions in the past, often by saying that a person was temporarily "possessed" by a spirit, ancestor, or god.

In graduate school I heard a story about a behavioral psychologist who was working on a multi-cultural IQ test and wanted to administer it to hunter-gatherers. I do not know if this story is true or not, I have unsuccessfully looked for it in the literature, so it may just be a parable. So the story goes, with the help of a cultural anthropologist the psychologist met a young hunter-gatherer boy and arranged for the test. When the boy arrived and realized what was going on he said, "I'll be back shortly" and left. He returned with his uncle and said, "We are ready for the test now". The psychologist explained that the test is meant to be taken individually and the young boy said, "Why would I do that when I have the knowledge and experience of my uncle available?" This clearly illustrates two starkly different approaches to the basic western concept of individuality and intelligence.

A Lot of Ancestors

If we arbitrarily establish a generation as twenty years (between one's birth and first child) then we have 5 generations in a century. Each generation doubles the number of direct ancestors we have. Two parents, four grandparents, eight great-grandparents and so forth. I originally did the math when I was a teenager and it did not take long to realize that within a few millennia we had more ancestors than there were people in any particular place on the face of the planet at the time, and hence, how small our original gene pool likely was.

This exponential progression is kind of like compound interest. There is a story that a reporter once asked Albert Einstein what the most powerful force in the universe was, and after thinking for a moment he said "compound interest". Here is (sort of) an example of this. A lobbyist friend borrowed a quarter from another friend for a phone call at the state capitol many years ago after a key vote (when all we had were pay phones). He promised to pay the quarter back at 100% interest per day, thinking he might owe 50 cents the next day, but the problem is he forgot. A year went by and the lender asked him to repay the loan. My friend reached into his pocket and said, "how much do I owe?" The lender smiled and said, correctly, "There is not enough money in the world for you to pay me back". I think they settled for a smaller amount.

So it goes with our ancestry. Most people can name some of their ancestors back maybe four or five generations but what about 3.6 million years' worth of ancestors at 5 generations per century? We did this exercise in class one semester. Using this scenario if you took your parents, then ONE ancestor from each generation and lined them up them side by side (assuming two feet shoulder-to-shoulder per ancestor) the lineup would stretch 360,000 feet, or about 68 miles. To understand your ancestry visually imagine getting in a car where you mom and dad are standing just next to you then driving down the road for 68 miles to the next city (like from Denver to Colorado Springs, Colorado). It would take that long to reach the beginning of your ancestry line, whizzing by your lined-up ancestors (one per generation) and that is just to the point of bipedalism. That is a lot of ancestors and after the first three miles they were all hunter-gatherers …

The Next Edition

If this book is well-received I will likely update it with photos that I can obtain permission to reprint and, convert place names to the local language, will correct and/or update any dates (300 or so), key topics and maybe add an index. I may find a professional proofreader too. I have several file drawers of additional information and examples to include, but I wanted to keep the book short for the non-specialist and so it was more about what to leave out than what to put in. My goal is to sell a few copies to people interested in this subject, (it would have been more if my mother was still alive) but a few will have to do.

I told myself that I would finish this book before July 2018 This last paragraph was finished at 7:11 PM (oddly enough) MDT on June 30, 2018.

At some point each story has to end so the next one can begin. Let the next one begin. But remember the best part is Chapter 20.

20 THE LAKH CLOCK

Most archaeology and history books include lots of dates (several hundred in this book) and they often represent them on a horizontal or vertical timeline of events (mostly horizontal). This provides a useful visual representation of when key things happened but there are always issues associated with scale that make the end result difficult to appreciate (we have to expand events in the last few thousand years) or it becomes jumbled..

I love timelines and have experimented with probably every possible way to visually represent the vast time of human prehistory and the major events, and they all fail due to the linear nature of the project.

After lots of experimentation I developed a representation that I call the "Lakh Clock" where every second in a 24 hour "day" equals one year. Interestingly, it is non-linear. One day therefore equals 86,400 years so everything ends up with a time reference on the circular clock that most people are accustomed to. I call it the "Lakh Clock" because Sanskrit has a word for 100,000 and it is close enough for me.

Due to rounding the "Lakh Time" equivalents below are generally accurate to plus or minus several years (where a second equals a year). What's a second in all of eternity? (paraphrasing a line from the 2017 movie *Beauty and the Beast*).

Here is the entire sequence of events from the narrative above (plus maybe a few more), converted to the "Lakh Clock" where "today" is 11:59 pm.

I calculated from 11:59 pm so that it would stay accurate for another 60 years which is one minute on the "Lakh Clock" and save everyone a lot of time. It is kind of like the problem associated with 1950 being (BP) in archaeology (discussed earlier).

I hope you enjoy this as much as I do, it really did take me several years to develop, and if there was someone who did it earlier I could not find it in the literature but will gladly defer to them as originators.

I am starting with the present and moving back, so you can see how things work. Not every recent date below is discussed in the narrative above. All dates are subject to revision because so much is happening in the field of archaeology. Keep informed by reading more.

As a friend of mine observed when he first saw this timeline, "Well, we've been up all day but the party really didn't get started until about 9:30 tonight". In a way he is right, this is when we see agriculture and domestication and the pace of change does increase dramatically.

Table 12. The Lakh Clock

Approx. Lakh Time	Key Event, Time Period, or Site	Approx. Date
11:59 PM	Today	
11:58 PM	Sputnik 1, Space Age Begins	1957
11:55 PM	British Colonize Australia as Penal Colony	1788
11:55 PM	James Cook Arrives in Hawaii	1778
11:55 PM	American Independence	1776
11:54 PM	Industrial Revolution Begins	1760
11:53 PM	James Ussher Calculates Age of World	1650
11:51 PM	Last Inca Emperor Executed	1572
11:51 PM	Protohistoric Period (N America)	1550
11:51 PM	Pizzaro Conquers Inca	1530
11:51 PM	Cortez Conquers Aztecs	1519
11:50 PM	Columbus Arrives in New World	1492

11:50 PM	Inca Empire	1476
11:50 PM	Portuguese Arrive in Sub Sahara Africa	1470
11:49 PM	Great Zimbabwe	1400
11:47 PM	New Zealand Colonized in Pacific	1280
11:46 PM	Hawaii Colonized in Pacific	1220
11:46 PM	Mongol Empire	1215
11:45 PM	Aztecs Arrive in Valley of Mexico	1200
11:45 PM	Easter Island Colonized in Pacific	1200
11:45 PM	Marquis Islands Colonized in Pacific	1200
11:45 PM	Angkor Thom – Cambodia	1181
11:44 PM	Chichen Itza Largely Abandoned (Mesoamerica)	1150
11:44 PM	Mesa Verde	1130
11:44 PM	Angkor Wat – Cambodia	1113
11:44 PM	Chimu Empire in North (Chan Chan) South America	1100
11:44 PM	Chimu Roadways	1100
11:44 PM	Hohokam Culture (American SW)	1100
11:43 PM	Chaco Phenomenon	1050
11:43 PM	Cahokia	1050
11:42 PM	Society Islands Colonized in Pacific	1025
11:42 PM	Bantu Migration to South Africa	1000
11:42 PM	Norse Settle Newfoundland	1000
11:42 PM	Islam Coastal Trade Ease Africa	1000
11:40 PM	Sican State (North) and Sea Trade (South America)	900
11:40 PM	Tikal Collapse (Mesoamerica)	869
11:39 PM	Jayaraman II – Cambodia Khmer Empire	802
11:39 PM	Kivas appear in American SW	800
11:38 PM	Teotihuacan Collapse	750
11:36 PM	Wari State (Andes and Coast of South America)	650
11:35 PM	Caracal Defeats Tikal (Mesoamerica)	562
11:34 PM	Amazon Chiefdoms (River Based)	500
11:34 PM	Teotihuacan Apex	500
11:33 PM	Copan Founded	435
11:33 PM	Palenque Founded	431
11:32 PM	Visigoths from Europe Sack Rome	410
11:32 PM	Roman Empire Splits in Two	395
11:31 PM	Constantine – Roman Christianity	313

THE LONG WALK HERE

11:29 PM	Tiwanaku State (South Andes) (South America)	200
11:25 PM	Anasazi (Ancestral Puebloans)	1
11:25 PM	Hopewell Mounds	1
11:25 PM	Formative Period Begins N Amer (generally)	1
11:25 PM	Extensive SE Asia Sea Trade	1
11:25 PM	Gregorian Calendar Start Date	1
11:25 PM	Roman Conquest of Egypt	30 BCE
11:24 PM	Julius Caesar Conquers Gaul	51 BCE
11:23 PM	Rome Destroys Carthage	146 BCE
11:22 PM	Nazca (South America)	200 BCE
11:22 PM	Moche State and Irrigation Agriculture (South America)	200 BCE
11:22 PM	Han Dynasty	206 BCE
11:21 PM	Emperor Akosa (India)	272 BCE
11:20 PM	Mogollon Culture (American SW)	300 BCE
11:20 PM	Mauryan Empire (India) Begins	319 BCE
11:20 PM	Alexander the Great Dies	323 BCE
11:20 PM	Alexander the Great India Campaign	326 BCE
11:20 PM	Chinese Empire Begins (Qin)	331 BCE
11:19 PM	Alexander the Great Conquers Egypt	343 BCE
11:19 PM	Monte Alban (Mesoamerica)	400 BCE
11:17 PM	Saladoid Migration to Bahamas	500 BCE
11:17 PM	La Tene Fortified Villages in Europe	500 BCE
11:17 PM	Persian Occupation of Egypt	525 BCE
11:16 PM	Cyrus the Great Annexes Babylon (Persia)	539 BCE
11:16 PM	Confucius	551 BCE
11:13 PM	Nubian Pharaohs	730 BCE
11:13 PM	Etruscans Fortify Rome	753 BCE
11:14 PM	Taino Settle Bahamas	700 BCE
11:14 PM	Adena Mounds in North America	700 BCE
11:12 PM	Mississippian Mounds in North America	800 BCE
11:10 PM	Ironworking in Africa	900 BCE
11:09 PM	Farming Communities Mesoamerican Lowlands	1,000 BCE
11:09 PM	Maize arrives in the Southeast Portion of North America)	1,000 BCE

11:09 PM	Villanovans Arrive in Mediterranean From Europe	1,000 BCE
11:09 PM	Ironworking in Europe	1,000 BCE
11:09 PM	Phoenicians	1,000 BCE
11:09 PM	Bronze in SE Asia	1,000 BCE
11:09 PM	Athens Florescence	1,000 BCE
11:09 PM	Cereal Cultivation in Sub-Sahara Africa	1,000 BCE
11:08 PM	Egypt Late Period	1,070 BCE
11:05 PM	Koster Occupation Ends (North America)	1,200 BCE
11:05 PM	Chinchorro Mummies (South America)	1,200 BCE
11:05 PM	Chavin de Huantar (South America)	1,200 BCE
11:05 PM	Rice in Philippines	1,200 BCE
11:05 PM	Olmec Culture (Mesoamerica)	1,200 BCE
11:04 PM	Ramses II	1,279 BCE
11:04 PM	Kadesh Peace Treaty (Hittite and Egypt)	1,286 BCE
11:03 PM	Tutankhamun	1,332 BCE
11:03 PM	Uluburun Shipwreck	1,320 BCE
11:02 PM	Assyrians Appear	1400 BCE
11:02 PM	Mycenaeans Appear	1400 BCE
11:00 PM	Ganges River Valley Development Begins	1,500 BCE
11:00 PM	Caral Abandoned (South America)	1,500 BCE
11:00 PM	Harrapan Civilization Disappears (Indus Valley)	1,500 BCE
11:00 PM	Woven Cotton, Pottery (South America)	1,500 BCE
11:00 PM	Egypt New Kingdom	1,530 BCE
10:59 PM	Lapita Culture in Pacific	1,550 BCE
10:58 PM	Egypt Second Intermediate Period	1,640 BCE
10:58 PM	Hittites Appear	1,650 BCE
10:57 PM	Thera Eruption (Minoan Decline)	1,700 BCE
10:54 PM	Early States in China (Xia), Bronze	1,900 BCE
10:52 PM	2nd Migration into Caribbean	2,000 BCE
10:52 PM	Pottery in Mesoamerica (Gourd Style)	2,000 BCE
10:52 PM	Maize Cultivation in the Southwest Portion of N America	2,000 BCE
10:52 PM	Earliest Millet Noodles (China)	2,000 BCE
10:52 PM	Urnfield Bronze in Europe	2,000 BCE

THE LONG WALK HERE

10:52 PM	Present Sahara Conditions (Africa)	2,000 BCE
10:52 PM	Minoan First Place Period	2,000 BCE
10:52 PM	Irrigation in Mesopotamia (Babylonians)	2,000 BCE
10:50 PM	Egypt Middle Kingdom	2,140 BCE
10:49 PM	Egypt First Intermediate Period	2,180 BCE
10:49 PM	Poverty Point in N America	2,200 BCE
10:47 PM	Akkadian Empire and Sargon	2,334 BCE
10:47 PM	Troy II	2,300 BCE
10:44 PM	Amesbury Archer in England from Europe	2,470 BCE
10:44 PM	Taro Cultivated in Pacific	2,500 BCE
10:44 PM	City of Mohenjo-daro in Indus Valley	2,500 BCE
10:43 PM	Great Pyramid of Egypt	2,528 BCE
10:43 PM	Egypt Old Kingdom	2,575 BCE
10:42 PM	Caral (city complex) in South America	2,627 BCE
10:40 PM	Bell Beaker Society in Europe – Trade	2,700 BCE
10:35 PM	Fortifications in China (Longshan)	3,000 BCE
10:35 PM	Farming Villages and Rice in SE Asia	3,000 BCE
10:35 PM	Cycladic Peoples	3.200 BCE
10:35 PM	Troy I	3.000 BCE
10:35 PM	Sumerian "Nascent World System"	3,000 BCE
10:35 PM	Cuneiform Appears (Mesopotamia)	3,000 BCE
10:35 PM	Wheeled Vehicles in Europe	3,000 BCE
10:34 PM	Egyptian State and Hieroglyphs	3,100 BCE
10:34 PM	Irrigation Agriculture in Egypt	3,100 BCE
10:34 PM	First Signs of Writing (Schmandt-Besserat (Mesopotamia)	3,100 BCE
10:33 PM	Mesoamerican Calendar "Start Date"	3,113 BCE
10:32 PM	Harrapan Civilization Rises in Indus Valley	3,200 BCE
10:31 PM	Scapula Writing in China (Liangzu)	3,250 BCE
10:29 PM	Otsi the Iceman (copper in Europe)	3,350 BCE
10:27 PM	Agriculture in Amazon	3,500 BCE
10:27 PM	Rice in Taiwan	3,500 BCE
10:27 PM	"First City" Uruk - Sumerians	3,500 BCE
10:25 PM	Plow Agriculture in Europe	3,600 BCE
10:22 PM	Signs of conflict at Tell Brak in Mesopotamia	3,800 BCE
10:19 PM	Earliest Occupants in Caribbean	4,000 BCE
10:19 PM	Sedentary Hunter Gatherers in Pacific NW	4,000 BCE

10:19 PM	Elites (Longshan) in China	4,000 BCE
10:19 PM	Flood Agriculture Well Established on Nile	4,000 BCE
10:19 PM	Agriculture in British Isles	4,000 BCE
10:19 PM	Proto Urban Towns (Kot Diji) in Indus Valley	4,000 BCE
10:19 PM	Fortified Villages in Anatolia	4,000 BCE
10:14 PM	Maize Possibly Domesticated (Mesoamerica)	4,300 BCE
10:10 PM	Earliest Coastal Textiles (South America)	4,500 BCE
10:10 PM	Sedentism in N Africa Established	4,500 BCE
10:10 PM	Megaliths Appear in France	4,500 BCE
10:02 PM	Yangshao – Millet Farmers in China	5,000 BCE
10:02 PM	Bankeramik Neolithic in Europe	5,000 BCE
10:02 PM	Gulf of Oman Reaches Current Level	5,000 BCE
9:46 PM	Agriculture Arrives in Nile from SW Asia	6,000 BCE
9:46 PM	Catalhoyuk Abandoned	6.000 BCE
9:45 PM	Neolithic in Southeast Europe and Coast	6,000 BCE
9:37 PM	Village Farming in North China	6,500 BCE
9:37 PM	Sahara is a Temperate Desert (unlike today)	6,500 BCE
9:37 PM	Britain Becomes an Island	6,500 BCE
9:37 PM	Rising Sea Levels Stabilize (roughly)	6,500 BCE
9:37 PM	Chiefdoms in Near East (Ubaid and Halafian)	6,500 BCE
9:29 PM	Inuit and Aleut in Arctic	7,000 BCE
9:29 PM	Rice Cultivation Well Established in China	7,000 BCE
9:29 PM	Mehgarh, Domesticated Cattle, Barley, Wheat, Cotton (Indus)	7,000 BCE
9:29 PM	Schmandt-Besserat (tokens appear)	7,000 BCE
9:20 PM	Koster Occupation Begins (N Amer)	7,500 BCE
9:21 PM	Catalhoyuk (Early)	7,500 BCE
9:12 PM	Rice Cultivation Begins (China)	8,000 BCE
9:12 PM	Ireland Becomes an Island	8.000 BCE
9:12 PM	Regional Trade in Obsidian and Other Materials (Near East)	8,000 BCE

THE LONG WALK HERE

9:12 PM	Bottle Gourds Possibly Domesticated (Mesoamerica)	8,020 BCE
9:11 PM	Herding and Small Farming in Zargos	8,500 BCE
9:04 PM	Hunter Gatherers in Amazon	8,500 BCE
9:04 PM	Villages and Farming in Fertile Crescent	8,500 BCE
8:59 PM	Cultivation of Wild Plants in Fertile Crescent	8,800 BCE
8:49 PM	Pottery in N Africa	9,400 BCE
8:47 PM	Archaic Period Generally Begins (N Amer)	9,500 BCE
8:44 PM	Younger Dryas Ends	9.650 BCE
8:44 PM	Gobekli Tepe	9,700 BCE
8:39 PM	Wild Rice Harvesting (China)	10,000 BCE
8:39 PM	"Neolithic" Begins, Jericho occupied (Mesopotamia)	10,000 BCE
8:39 PM	Jericho Occupied, Late Natufian	10,000 BCE
8:23 PM	Younger Dryas Begins	10,950 BCE
8:19 PM	Clovis Big Game Hunters	11,200 BCE
8:22 PM	Holocene Begins	11,000 BCE
8:06 PM	Paleoindian Period (New World)	12,000 BCE
7:57 PM	Jomon Pottery (Japan)	12,500 BCE
7:55 PM	Early Natufian	12,600 BCE
7:37 PM	Warming Period Begins	13,700 BCE
7:28 PM	Monte Verde (South America)	14,220 BCE
7:15 PM	Glacial Maximum	17,000 years ago
7:17 PM	*Homo floresiensis* Disappears	17,000 years ago
7:00 PM	Humans Reach North America (roughly)	18,000 years ago
5:01 PM	Neanderthals Disappear (roughly)	25,000 years ago
3:07 PM	Dogs Domesticated (perhaps)	32,000 years ago
3:07 PM	Chauvet Rock Art	32,000 years ago
1:42 PM	New Guinea Settled	35,000 years ago
12:53 PM	Hohenstein Stadel (Lion Man Figure)	40,000 years ago

11:30 AM	Humans Colonize Australia by Sea (estimate)	45,000 years ago
10:07 AM	Denisovans Appear	50,000 years ago
12:00 AM	Modern Human Behavior (roughly)	86,400 years ago
Yesterday	*Homo floresiensis* Appears	95,000 years ago
2 days ago	Neanderthals Appear (roughly)	150,000 years ago
2.3 days ago	Anatomically Modern Humans Appear	200,000 years ago
3 days ago	Controlled Use of Fire (roughly)	250,000 years ago
3.5 days ago	Schoningen Spears	300,000 years ago
4 days ago	*Homo naledi*	335,000 years ago
7 days ago	*Homo heidelbergenesis*	600,000 years ago
20 days ago	Language (inferred)	1.7 million years ago
20 days ago	*Homo erectus* Appears	1.7 million years ago
20 days ago	*Homo ergaster* Appears	1.7 million years ago
20 days ago	Pleistocene Begins	1.8 million years ago
Three weeks ago	Genus *Homo* appears (*H. habilis*)	2 million years ago
Three weeks ago	Australopithecines disappear	2 million years ago
Three weeks ago	First Stone Tools (more or less)	2.2 million years ago
A month and a half ago	Bipedalism	3,600,000 years ago
Two months ago	Pliocene Epoch Begins	5,300,000 years ago
Two months ago	Humans and Chimps Split (est.)	6,000,000 years ago
Three months ago	Humans and Chimps Split (est.)	8,000,000 years ago

One year ago	Primate Dispersal	23,000,000 years ago
Just over a year ago	Primates Appear	33,900,000 years ago
Two years ago	Dinosaurs Extinct	65 million years ago
146 years ago	Earth Formed	4.6 billion years ago
438 years ago	Big Bang	13.8 billion years ago

REFERENCES

Ackermann, Rebecca Rogers and Richard J. Smith. 2007. The Macroevolution of our Ancient Lineage: What We Know (or Think We Know) about Early Hominin Diversity. *Evolutionary Biology* 34: 72085.

Adams, Robert M. 1966. *The Evolution of Urban Society*. Aldine, Chicago.

Adler, Michael. 2002. Negotiating the Village. Community Landscapes in the Late Pre-Historic American Southwest. In *Inscribed Landscapes: Marking and Making Place*, edited by Bruno David and Meredith Wilson, pp. 200-216. University of Hawaii Press, Honolulu.

Alcock, Susan E. and John F. Cherry. 2013. "Chapter 13 The Mediterranean World." In *The Human Past, 3rd edition*. Chris Scarre, ed. pp 200-231. Thames and Hudson, London.

Algaze, Guillermo. 2001. Initial Social Complexity in Southwestern Asia: The Mesopotamian Advantage. *Current Anthropology* 42:199-215.

Andrefsky, Jr., William. 2005. *Lithic: Macroscopic Approaches to Analysis, 2nd Edition*. University of Cambridge Press, Cambridge.

Armstrong, Karen. 2014. *Fields of Blood: Religion and the History of Violence*. Anchor Books, New York.

Archer, Margaret (ed) and Roy Bhaskar, Andrew Collier, Tony Lawson and Alan Norrie. 1998. *Critical Realism*. Routledge, New York.

Arnold, Jeanne E. 1992. Complex Hunter-Gatherer-Fishers of Prehistoric California: Chiefs, Specialists, and Maritime Adaptations of the Channel Island. *American Antiquity* 57:60-84.

Aveni, Anthony. 2009. *The End of Time. The Maya Mystery of 2012*. University Press of Colorado, Boulder.

Babbie, E. 2004. *The Practice of Social Research*. Thompson, Belmont. Pp 32-60.

Bahn, Paul G. (ed). 1996. *Cambridge Illustrated History (of) Archaeology*. Cambridge University Press, New York.

Bahn, Paul G. (ed). 2014. *The History of Archaeology: An Introduction*. Routledge, Oxon.

Balter, Michael. 2014a. The Killing Ground. Clues from a German coal mine show how early hunters lived, 30,000 years ago, and how their prey died. *Science*, vol 344: 1080-1083.

Balter, Michael. 2014b. RIP for a key Homo species? *Science*, vol 345: 129.

Balter, Michael. 2014c. Monumental Roots. *Science*. 3 January 2014, vol 343, pp 18-23.

Balter, Michael. 2005. *The Goddess and The Bull. Çatalhöyük: An Archaeological Journey to the Dawn of Civilization*. Free Press, New York.

Bar-Yosef, Offer. 1998. The Natufian culture in the Levant, threshold to the origins of agriculture. *Evolutionary Anthropology*, 6(5), 159-177.

Barber, Gary (et. al.) (Producer), Jennings, Garth (Director), 2005. *Hitchhiker's Guide to the Galaxy* (Motion Picture). Touchstone Pictures.

Bawaya, Michael. 2014. A chocolate habit in ancient North America. *Science*, 345:991.

Beekman, Christopher S. 2010. Recent Research in Western Mexican Archaeology. *Journal of Archaeological Research*, 18:41-109.

Bellwood, Peter and Peter Hiscock. 2013. "Chapter 8 Australia and the Pacific Basin During the Holocene." In *The Human Past, 3rd edition*. Chris Scarre, ed. pp 265-305. Thames and Hudson, London.

Bender, Barbara. 1998. Prehistoric Landscapes of Stonehenge. Ch 2 from *Stonehenge. Making Space*. Berg Publishers, Oxford. Pp. 39-67.

Bender, Barbara. 1981. Gatherer-Hunter Intensification. In *Economic Archaeology*, edited by A. Sheridan and G. Bailey, pp.; 149-157. BAR International Series 96, London.

Bernard, H. Russell. 2002. *Research Methods in Anthropology, Qualitative and Quantitative Methods*. 3rd edition. Altamira press, Walnut Creek.

Bestman, Catherine & Hugh Gusterson, (eds). 2005. *Why America's Top Pundits are Wrong: Anthropologists Talk Back*. University of California Press, Berkeley.

Binford, Lewis. 1966. A Preliminary Analysis of Functional Variability in the Mousterian of Levallois Facies. *American Anthropologist*, vol 68, no. 2 part 2: 238-295.

Binford, L. R. 1962. Archaeology as Anthropology. *American Antiquity* 28: 217-225.

Bird-David, Nurit. 1992. Beyond "The Original Affluent Society": A Culturalist Reformulation. In *Limited Wants, Unlimited Means, A Reader on Hunter-Gatherer Economics and the Environment*, edited by John Gowdy, pp. 115-138, Island Press, Washington, DC.

Blades, Brooke S. 2003. End Scraper Reduction and Hunter-Gatherer Mobility. *American Antiquity*, vol. 68(1): 141-156.

Blanton, Richard E. et al. 1996. A Dual-Processual Theory for the Evolution of Mesoamerican Civilization. *Current Anthropology* 37:1-14

Boyd, Richard, Philip Gasper, and J. D. Trout (eds). 1999. *The Philosophy of Science*. MIT Press, Cambridge, Massachusetts.

Braidwood, R.J., and L. S. Braidwood, eds. 1983. Prehistoric Archaeology along the Zargos Flanks. Oriental Institute. Chicago.

Brauer, Gunter. 2008. The Origin of Modern Anatomy: By Speciation or Intraspecific Evolution? *Evolutionary Anthropology*, 17:22-37.

Browman, David L, Gayle J Fritz, Patty Jo Watson, and David J. Meltzer. 2013. "Chapter 9 Origins of Food-Producing Economies in the Americas." In *The Human Past, 3rd edition*.

Chris Scarre, ed. pp 306-349. Thames and Hudson, London.

Bruner, E. 2004. Evolution, actuality and species concept: A need for a paleontological tool. *Human Evolution* 19:93-112.

Bryson, Bill. 1998. *A Walk in The Woods*. Broadway Books, Broadway, New York

Bryson, Bill. 2003. *A Short History of Nearly Everything*. Broadway Books, Broadway, New York.

Buikstra, Jane E. and Douglas K. Charles. 1999. Centering the Ancestors: Cemeteries, Mounds and Sacred Landscapes of the Ancient North American Midcontinent. In *Archaeologies of Landscape. Contemporary Perspectives*, edited by Wendy Ashmore and A. Bernard Knapp, pp. 201-228. Blackwell Publishers, Oxford.

Carnerio, Robert L. 1970. A Theory of the Origin of the State. *Science* 169: 733-738.

Cartmill, M. 1999. The status of the race concept in physical anthropology. American Anthropologist 100: 632-650.

Cassells, E. Steve. 1997. *The Archaeology of Colorado*. Revised Edition. Johnson Books, Boulder.

Chauvet, Jean-Marie (et al.) 1996. *Dawn of Art: The Chauvet Cave*. Harry N. Abrams, Inc. New York.

Childe, V. G. 1971. The Neolithic revolution. *Prehistoric Agriculture* pp. 15-21. Natural history press, New York.

Childe, V. G. 1950. The urban revolution. *Town Planning Review*, 21(1), p.3.

Clark, John E. and Michael Blake. 1994. The Power of Prestige: Competitive Generosity and the Emergence of Rank Societies in Lowland Mesoamerica. In *Factional Competition and Political Development in the New World*, edited by E. M. Brumfiel and J. E. Fox, pp. 15-30. Cambridge University Press, Cambridge.

Cohen, Mark. 1977. The Food Crisis in Prehistory. Yale University Press. New Haven.

Coulter, Dauna. 2009. The Fall of the Maya: They Did it to Themselves. *NASA Science Beta*. https://science.nasa.gov/science-news/science-at-nasa/2009/06oct_maya. Accessed 16 July 2017.

Connah, Graham. 2013. "Chapter 10 Holocene Africa." In *The Human Past, 3rd edition*. Chris Scarre, ed. pp 350391. Thames and Hudson, London.

Cowgill, George L. 2004. Origins and Development of Urbanism: Archaeological Perspectives. *Annual Review of Anthropology* 33: 525-549.

Conningham, Robin. 2013. "Chapter 14 South Asia: From Early Villages to Buddhism." In *The Human Past, 3rd edition*. Chris Scarre, ed. pp 350-391. Thames and Hudson, London.
Cron, Lisa. 2012. *Wired for Story*. Ten Speed Press, Berkeley.

Crumley, Carole L. 1995. Heterarchy and the analysis of complex societies. In Heterarchy and the analysis of complex societies, edited by Robert M. Ehrenreich, Carole L. Crumley, and Janet E. Levy, pp 1-5. *Archaeological Papers of the American Anthropological Association*, No 6. Washington, DC.

Cunliffe, Barry. 2008. *Europe Between the Oceans: 9000 BCE to AD 1000*. London & New Haven: Yale University Press.

Curtis, Gregory. 2006. *The Cave Painters: Probing the Mysteries of the Word's First Artists*. Anchor Books, New York.

Dales, G.F. 1964. *The mythical massacre at Mohenjodaro*. Expedition 6:36-43.

Damasio, Antonio. 1994. *Descartes's Error: Emotion, Reason, and the Human Brain*. Penguin, New York.

DeSalle, Rob and Ian Tattersalll. 2008. *Human Origins*. Nevaurmont Publishing Company, Bronx, New York.

Demarest, Arthur A. 1992. Ideology in Ancient Maya Cultural Evolution: The Dynamics of Galactic Polities. In Ideology and Pre-Columbian Civilizations, edited by A. A. Demarest and G. W. Conrad, pp. 135-157. School of American Research, Santa Fe.

Diamond, Jared. 2013. *The World Until Yesterday*. Penguin Books, New York.

Dobzhansky, T. 1944 *American Journal of Physical Anthropology* 2, 25. Cited in Schwars, Jeffrey H. and Ian Tattersall, "Defining the genus Homo", *Science*, 2015, vol 349: 931-932.

Dobzhansky, Theodosius. 1962. Mankind Evolving: *The Evolution of Human Species*. Yale University Press, Connecticut.

Durkheim, Emile. 1995 (1912). *The Elementary Forms of Religious Life (A New Translation by Karen E. Fields)*. The Free Press, New York.

Fairclough, Graham. 1999. Protecting time and space: understanding historic landscape for conservation in England. In *The Archaeology and Anthropology of Landscape. Shaping Your Landscape,* edited by Pter J. Ucko and Robert Layton, pp. 119-134. One World Archaeology Series, Routledge, London.

Fagan, Brian and Nadia Durrani. 2014. *People of the Earth, 14th edition*. Pearson, Boston.

Fagan, Brian M. 2010. *Ancient Lives: An Introduction to Archaeology and Prehistory, 4th ed.* Prentice Hall, New Jersey.

Feder, Kenneth L. 2008. *Linking to the Past. A Brief Introduction to Archaeology, 2nd edition*. Oxford University Press, New York.

Feder, Kenneth L. 2007. *The Past in Perspective. An Introduction to Human Prehistory, 4th edition*. McGraw Hill, Boston.

Feigl, Herbert. 1988. The Scientific Outlook: Naturalism and Humanism. In Introductory Readings in the Philosophy of Science, Edited by E. D. Klemke et al., pp 427-437. Prometheus Books, Buffalo.

Fitzhugh, William W. and Morris Rossabi and William Honeychurch (eds). 2009. *Gengis Khan and the Mongul Empire*. Dino Don, Inc, University of Washington Press.

Flannery, Kent V. 1972. "The Cultural Evolution of Civilizations." *Annual Review of Ecology and Systemics* 4: 399-426.

Flannery, K. V. 1967. Culture History vs. Culture Process: A Debate in American Archaeology. *Scientific American* 217: 119-122.

Gluck, Andrew. 2007. *Damasio's Error and Descartes' Truth*. University of Scranton Press, Scranton, New Jersey.

Fox, John W. et al. 1996. *Questions of Political and Economic Integration: Segmentary versus Centralized States Among the Ancient Maya*. Current Anthropology 37:795-801.

Friedman, Jonathan. 1979. *System, Structure, and Contradiction: The Evolution of "Asiatic" social Formations*. Cambridge University Press, Cambridge.

Frahm, Ellery and Joshuma M. Feinberg. 2013. Environment and collapse: Eastern Anatolian obsidians at Urkesh (Tell Mozan, Syria) and the third-millennium Mesopotamian urban crisis. In *Journal of Archaeological Science*. Vol. 40 (2013) pp. 1866-1878.

Fritz, Sandy. 2000. Who Was the Iceman?" *In Exploring the Past: Readings in Archaeology*. James M. Bayman and Miriam T. Stark, eds. pp 211-217. Carolina Academic Press, Durham.

Gibbon, E. 1804. *The history of the decline and fall of the Roman Empire*. (vol 5). William Y. Birch & Abraham Small, Printed by Robert Carr.

Gibbons, Ann. 2017. Neandertals mated early with modern humans. *Science*. 7 July 2017. Vol 356: 14.

Gibbons, Ann. 2015. Deep roots for the genus Homo. *Science*. 6 March 2015, Vol 347: 1056-1057.

Gibbons, Ann. 2014. Neanderthals and moderns made imperfect mates. *Science*. 31 January 2014. Vol 343: 471-472.

Goldenberg, Sheldon. 1992. *Thinking Methodologically*. Harper Collins, New York.

Gottschall, Jonathan. 2012. *The Storytelling Animal: How Stories Make Us Human*. Houghton Mifflin Harcourt, Boston.

Gowdy, John (ed). 1998. *Limited Wants, Unlimited Means, A Reader on Hunter-Gatherer Economics and the Environment*. Island Press, Washington, DC.
Grimm, David. 2015. Dawn of the Dog. *Science*. 17 April 2015, vol 348: 274-279.

Groves, C. 2004. The What, Why and How of Primate Taxonomy. *International Journal of Primatology*, vol. 25 (5): 1105-1125.

Hawass, Zahi. n/d. *Tutankhamun: The Golden King and the Great Pharaohs*. National Geographic, Washington, DC.

Hayden, Brian. 2011. Feasting and Social Dynamics in the Epipaleolithic of the Fertile Crescent: An Interpretive Exercise. In *Guess Who's Coming to Dinner: Feasting rituals in the prehistoric societies of Europe and the Near East*. Jimenez, G. A., Monton-Subiad, D., & Sanchez Romero, M. (eds.), 30-63. Oxbow Books, Oxford.

Hayden, Brian. 2003. "A New overview of Domestication." In Last Hunters-first Farmers. T.D. Price and A.B. Gebauer, eds. Pp. 273-299. School of American Research, Santa Fe.

Haviland, William T. 2002. *Cultural Anthropology 10th edition*. Wadsworth.

Higham, Charles. 2013. "Chapter 15 Complex Societies of East and Southeast Asia." In *The Human Past, 3rd edition*. Chris Scarre, ed. pp 552-593. Thames and Hudson, London.

Herzog, Werner. 2010. *Cave of Forgotten Dreams*. Erik Neilson Producer. Ministre de la Culture et de la communication Arte France

Hodder, Ian. 2006. The Leopard's Tale. *Revealing the Mysteries of Çatalhöyük*. Thames & Hudson, New York.

Hodder, Ian and Craig Cessford. 2004. Daily Practice and Social Memory at Çatalhöyük. In *American Antiquity*, Vol. 69, No. 1 (Jan 2004), pp. 17-40.

Hodder, Ian. 1982. Theoretical Archaeology: A Reactionary View. In *Symbolic and Structural Archaeology*, edited by Ian Hodder, pp. 1-16. Cambridge University Press, Cambridge.

Hodder, Ian. 1991a. Interpretive Archaeology and its Role. *American Antiquity*, vol. 56: 7-18.

Hodder, Ian. 1991b. Postprocessual archaeology and the current debate. *In Processual and Post-Processual Archaeologies: Multiple Ways of Knowing the Past*, edited by R. W. Preucel, pp. 30-41. Center for Archaeological Investigations, Southern Illinois University at Carbondale, Occasional Paper No. 10.

Hoest, Bill. *Quotations Page*. www.quotationspage.com/quote/818.html. Accessed 30 April 2017.

Holtorf, Cornelius J. 1997. Megaliths, Monumentality, and Memory. *Archaeological Review from Cambridge* 14(2): 45-66.

Hough, Richard. 1997. *Captain James Cook. A Biography*. W.W. Norton & Company, Inc., New York.

Hales, C. Nicholas and David J. P. Barker. 2001. The thrifty phenotype hypothesis. British Medical Bulletin 60:5-20.

Hole, Frank. 1994. "Environmental Instabilities and Urban Origins." In *Chiefdoms and Early States in the Near East: The Organizational Dynamics of Complexity*. G. Stein and M. S. Rothman, eds. Pp. 121-143. Prehistory Press, Madison.

Holen, Steven R. and Kathleen Holen. 2013. The mammoth steppe hypothesis: The middle Wisconsin (oxygen isotope state 3) peopling of North America. In *Paleoamerican Odyssey* 429-444.

Hublin, Jean-Jacques. 2014. How to build a Neandertal. Fossils from Sima de los Huesos show a mixture of Neandertal and more ancient features. *Science*. 2014. 20 June 2014. Vol 344:1338-1339.

Iseminger, William. 2010. *Cahokia Mounds: America's First City*. The History Press, Charleston.

James, William. 2004 (1902). *The Varieties of Religious Experience* (with Introduction and Notes by Wayne Proudfoot). Barnes and Noble Classics, New York.

Jacob, T., E. Indriati, R.P. Sojono, K. Hsu, D. W. Frayer, R. B. Eckhards, A. J. Kuperavage, and A. Thorne. 2006. Pygmoid Australomelanesian *Homo sapiens* skeletal remains from Liang Bua, Flores: Population affinities and pathological abnormalities. *Proceedings of the National Academy of Sciences*, vol 103(36): 13421-13426.

Jansen, M. 1989. Water Supply and Sewage Disposal at Mohenjo-Daro. World Archaeology, Vol. 21, No. 2. Pp 177-192.

Johnson, Jeffrey C. 1998. Research Design and Research Strategies. In *Handbook of Methods in Cultural Anthropology*, edited by H. R. Bernard, pp. 131-171. Alta Mira Press, Walnut Creek.

Kachigan, Sam Kash. 1986. *Statistical Analysis: An Interdisciplinary Introduction to Univariate and Multivariate Methods*. Radius Press, New York.

Keene, Arthur S. 1981. Optimal foraging in a nonmarginal environment: A Model of prehistoric subsistence strategies in Michigan. In *Hunter-Gatherer Foraging Strategies: Ethnographic and Archaeological Analyses*, edited by B. Winterhalder and E.A. Smith, pp 171-193. University of Chicago Press.

Kelly, Robert. 1983. Hunter-Gatherer Mobility Strategies. *Journal of Anthropological Research* 39(3): 277-306.

Kemp, Barry. 2005. *Ancient Egypt: The Anatomy of a Civilization*, 2nd ed. Routelege, London.
Kennedy, Kathleen and Gerald R. Modem (Producers), Spielberg, Steven (Director). 1993. *Jurassic Park*. Universal Pictures

Kierkegaard, Soren. nd. BrainyQuote.com, Xplore Inc, 2018. https://www.brainyquote.com/quotes/soren_kierkegaard_105030, accessed April 29, 2018.

Kirch, Partick Vinton. 2010. *How Chiefs Became Kings*. University of California Press, Berkeley and Los Angeles.

Kissinger, Henry. 2014. *World Order*. Penguin Books, New York. Also see *The Week*, September 26, 2014, Book of the Week, Review of reviews: Books, p. 21.

Klein, Richard. 2018. "Chapter 3 Hominin Dispersals in the Old World" In *The Human Past*, 4rd *edition*. Chris Scarre, ed. pp 104-105. Thames and Hudson, London.

Kotler Philip, 1991. Marketing Management, 7th ed. Prentice-Hall, Inc., New Jersey.

Kroeber, A.L. and C. Kluckhohn. 1952. *Culture: A Critical Review of Concepts and Definitions*. *Peabody Museum*, Cambridge.

Kuhn, Thomas S. 1970. *The Structure of Scientific Revolutions, 2nd ed.* University of Chicago, Chicago.

Leakey. Richard. 1994. *The Origin of Humankind.* Basic Books, New York.

LeBlanc, Steven A. and Katherine E. Register. 2003. *Constant Battles: The Myth of the Peaceful, Noble Savage.* St. Martin's Press, New York.

Lee, Richard B. 1968[1998]. What Hunters Do for a Living, or, How to Make Out on Scarce Resources. In *Limited Wants, Unlimited Means, A Reader on Hunter-Gatherer Economics and the Environment,* edited by John Gowdy, pp. 43-64, Island Press, Washington, DC.

Lehner, Mark. 1997. *The Complete Pyramids.* Thames & Hudson, London.

Louden, Robert B. (ed). 2006. *Anthropology from a Pragmatic Point of View.* Cambridge University Press.

McGuire, Randall H. and Dean J. Saitta. Although they Have Petty Captains, They Obey them Badly: The Dialectics of Prehispanic Western Pueblo Social Organization. *American Antiquity*, 61:197-216.

MacQuire, Kim. 2017. *The Last Days of the Incas.* Simon & Schuster, New York.

Marean, Curtis W. et al. 2007. Early human use of marine resources and pigment in South Africa during the Middle Pleistocene. *Nature*, vol. 449: 905-909.

Martin, Curtis. 2016. *Ephemeral Bounty: Wickiups, Trade Goods, and the Final Years of the Autonomous Ute.* University of Utah Press, Salt Lake City.

Martin, P. S. 1984. Prehistoric overkill: the global model. In *Quaternary Extinctions: A Prehistoric Revolution.* Martin, P. S. & Klein, r. G. (eds), pp. 354-403. University of Arizona Press, Tucson.

Matthews, Roger. 2013. "Chapter 12 Peoples and Complex Societies of Ancient Southwest Asia." In *The Human Past, 3rd edition.* Chris Scarre, ed. pp 432-471. Thames and Hudson, London.

McGlone, Matt. 2012. The Hunters Did It: Human hunting was responsible for the extinction of large mammal species in tropical Australia. *Science.* 23 March 2012, vol 335 pp 1452-1453

McGuire, Randall H. and Dean J. Saitta. 1996. Although They Have Petty Captains, They Obey them Badly: The Dialectics of Prehispanic Western Pueblo Social Organization. American Antiquity 61:197-216.

McIntosh, Jane R. 2008. *The Ancient Indus Valley: New Perspectives.* ABCE-CLIO, Santa Barbara.

Mellars, Paul. 2005. The Impossible Coincidence. A Single-Species Model for the Origins of Modern Human Behavior in Europe. 2005. *Evolutionary Anthropology*, 14: 12-27.

Milner, George R. and W. H. Wills. 2013. "Chapter 18 Complex Societies of North America." In the Americas." In *The Human Past, 3rd edition*. Chris Scarre, ed. pp 678-715. Thames and Hudson, London.

Mink, Claudia Gellman. 1992. *Cahokia City of the Sun*. Cahokia Mounds Museum Society, Collinsville, Illinois.

Mitchell, Stephen. 2004. *Gilgamesh*. A New English Version. Free Press, New York, New York.

Mithen, Steven. 2006. *The Singing Neanderthals: The Origins of Music, Language, Mind and Body*. Harvard University Press, Cambridge.

Mosimann, James and Paul S. Martin. 1975. Simulating Overkill by Paleoindians: Did man hunt the giant mammals of the New World to extinction? *American Scientist*, Vol. 63, No. 3, pp. 304-313).

Moseley, Michael e. and Michael J. Heckenberger. 2013. "Chapter 17 From Village to Empire in South America." In *The Human Past, 3rd edition*. Chris Scarre, ed. pp 640-677. Thames and Hudson, London.

Nance, J. D. 1987. Reliability, Validity, and Quantitative methods in Archaeology. In *Quantitative Methods in Archaeology*, edited by M. Aldenderfer, pp. 224-293. Sage, Beverly Hills.

Neel, James V. 1999(1962). Diabetes Mellitus: A "Thrifty" Genotype Rendered Detrimental by "Progress"? *American Journal of Human Genetics* 14:353-362.

Odell, George H. 2004. *Lithic Analysis*. Springer Science+Business LLC, New York.

Omohundro, John T. 2008. *Thinking Like an Anthropologist: A Practical Introduction to Cultural Anthropology*. McGraw-Hill, New York.

Papagianni, Mimitra and Michael A. Morse. 2013. *The Neanderthals Rediscovered: How Modern Science is Rewriting Their Story*. Thames and Hudson, London.

Patton, Michael Quinn. 2002. *Qualitative Research & Evaluation Methods*. Sage Publications, London.

Peterson, Jane. 1998. The Natufian Hunting Conundrum: Spears, Atlatls, or Bows? Musculoskeletal and Armature Evidence. *International Journal of Osteoarchaeology*, 8: 378-389.

Possehl, Gregory L. 2003. *Indus Civilization: A Conterporary Perspective*. AltiMira Press, Walnut Creek, CA

Rader, Melvin. 1976. *The Enduring Questions*. Holt, Rinehart and Winston, New York, New York.

Rappaport, Roy A. 1999. *Ritual and Religion in the Making of Humanity*. Cambridge University Press, Cambridge.

Reeves, Nicholas. 1990. *The Complete Tutankhamun*. Thames and Hudson, New York.

Renfrew, Colin and Paul Bahn. 2008. *Archaeology: Theories, Methods and Practice.* Thames and Hudson, London.

Renfrew, Colin and Paul Bahn. 2010. *Archaeology Essentials 2nd Edition.* Thames & Hudson, London.

Rice, Glen and Charles Redman. 1993. Platform Mounds of the Arizona Desert: An Experiment in Organizational Complexity. *Expedition,* 35(1):53063.

Robinson, Andrew. 2007. *The Story of Writing: Alphabets, Hieroglyphs & Pictograms.* Thames & Hudson, London.

Rowe, Christopher. 2005. *Plato's Phaedrus.* Penguin Classics, Penguin Group, New York, New York.

Sahlins, Marshall. 1972[1998]. The Original Affluent Society. In *Limited Wants, Unlimited Means, A Reader on Hunter-Gatherer Economics and the Environment,* edited by John Gowdy, pp. 5-42, Island Press, Washington, DC.

Sankararaman, Sriram, Swapan Mallick, Michael Adnnemann, Kay Frufer, Janet Kelso, Svante Paablo, Nick Paterson, David Reich. The genomic landscape of Neanderthal ancestry in present-day humans. *Nature,* 507:354-357.

Scarre, Chris. 2013a. *The Human Past, 3rd edition.* Chris Scarre, ed. Thames and Hudson, London.

Scarre, Chris. 2013b. "Chapter 5 The World Transformed: From Foragers and Farmers to States and Empires." In *The Human Past, 3rd edition.* Chris Scarre, ed. pp 176-199. Thames and Hudson, London.

Scarre, Chris. 2013c. "Chapter 11 Holocene Europe." In *The Human Past, 3rd edition.* Chris Scarre, ed. pp 392-431. Thames and Hudson, London.

Schmandt-Besserat, D. 1992. *Before Writing.* University of Texas Press, Austin.

Schmandt-Besserat, D. 1981. "Decipherment of the Earliest Tablets." *Science* 211:283-284.

Scott, James C. 2017. *Against the Grain. A Deep History of the Earliest States.* Yale University Press, New Haven.

Service, Wlman. 1962. *Primitive Social Organization.* Random House, New York.

Semaw, Sileshi. 2000. The World's Oldest Stone Artefacts from Gona, Ethiopia: Their Implications for Understanding Stone Technology and Patterns of Human Evolution Between 2.6-1.5 Million Years Ago. *Journal of Archaeological Science,* 27: 1197-1214.

Shepard, Paul. 1992. A Post-Historic Perspective. In *Limited Wants, Unlimited Means, A Reader on Hunter-Gatherer Economics and the Environment,* edited by John Gowdy, Island Press, Washington, DC.

Simmons, Annette. 2007. *Whoever Tells the Best Story Wins.* American Management Association, New York.

Smalley, John and Michael Blake. 2003. Sweet Beginnings. Stalk Sugar and the Domestication of Maize. *Current Anthropology*, 44: 675-703.

Smith, Adam T. 2003. *The Political Landscape. Constellations of Authority in Early Complex Polities*. University of California Press, Berkeley.

Smith, Adam T. 2000. Rendering the Political Aesthetic: Political Legitimacy in Uraritan Representations of the Built Environment. *Journal of Anthropological Archaeology* 119:131-163.

Smith, Bruce D. 1998. *The Emergence of Agriculture*. 2nd ed. Freeman. New York.

Snead, James E. 2002. Ancestral Pueblo Trails and the Cultural Landscape of the Pajarito Plateau, New Mexico. *Antiquity* 76(293): 756-765.

Stanford, Dennis J. and Bruce A. Bradley. 2012. *Across Atlantic Ice. The Origin of America's Clovis Culture*. University of California Press. Berkeley.

Stringer, Chris. 2012. *Lone Survivors*. Henry Holt and Company LLC, New York, New York.

Tattersall, Ian. 2000. Paleoanthropology: The Last Half-Century. *Evolutionary Anthropology*, Special Article, 2-16.

Sussman, R.W. 1999. The Taxonomy and Evolution of Primates. In R. W. Sussman (ed), *The Biological Basis of Human Behavior: A Critical Review*. Prentice Hall, Saddle River.

Tainter, Joseph. 1988. *The Collapse of Civilizations*. Cambridge University Press, Cambridge.

Tattersall, Ian. 2012. *Masters of the Planet: The Search for Our Human Origins*. Palgrave MacMillan, New York.

Templeton, Alan. 1999. Human Races: A Genetic and Evolutionary Perspective. *American Anthropologist* 100:632-650.

Thomas, David Hurst. 1976. *Figuring Anthropology: First Principles of Probability and Statistics*. Holt, Rinehart and Winston, New York.

Tilley, Christopher. 1996. The powers of rocks: Topography and monument construction on Bodmin Moor. *World Archaeology* 28: 161-176.

Tilley, Christopher. 1990. Michel Foucault: Towards an Archaeology of Archaeology. In *Reading Material Culture. Structuralism, Hermeneutics, and Post-Structuralism*, edited by Christopher Tilley. Basil Blackwell, Oxford.

Van Dyke, Ruth M. 2004. Memory, Meaning, and Masonry: The Late Bonito Chacoan Landscape. *American Antiquity* 69(3): 413-431

Varki, Ajit and Danny Brower. 2013. *Denial. Self-Deception, False Beliefs, and the Origins of the Human Mind*. Twelve, Hachette Book Group, New York, New York.

Waguespack, Nicole M. 2007. Why We're Still Arguing About the Pleistocene Occupation of the Americas. *Evolutionary Anthropology*, vol. 16: 63-74.

Waguespack, Nicole M. 2003. Clovis Hunting Strategies, or How to Make out on Plentiful Resources. *American Antiquity*, vol. 68(2): 333-352.

Walters, Matt. 2014. *Ancient Persia. A Concise History of the Achaemenid Empire, 550-330 BCEE*. Cambridge University Press, New York, New York.

Watkins, Trevor. 2013. "Chapter 6 From Foragers to Complex Societies in Southwest Asia." In *The Human Past, 3rd edition*. Chris Scarre, ed. pp 200-231. Thames and Hudson, London.

Webster, David. 2002. *The Fall of the Ancient Maya: Solving the Mystery of the Maya Collapse*. Thames & Hudson, London.

Wenke, Robert J. and Deborah I. Olszewski. 2007. *Patterns in Prehistory, 5th edition*. Oxford University Press, Inc., Oxford.

Whittaker, John C. 1994. *Flintknapping: Making and Understanding Stone Tools*. University of Texas Press, Austin.

Wilkinson, Tony J. 2003. Elements of Landscape. Ch. 4 from *Archaeological Landscapes of the Near East*. University of Arizona Press, Tucson. Pp. 44-70.

Wobst, H. M. 1978. The archaeo-ethnology of hunter-gatherers, or the tyranny of the ethnographic record in archaeology. *American Antiquity* 43: 303-309.

Wrangham, Richard. 2009. *Catching Fire: How Cooking Made Us Human*. Basic Books, New York.

Wright, Henry T. 1978. Toward an explanation of the origin of the state. In *Origins of the State. The Anthropology of Political Evolution*, edited by Roland Cohen and Elman R. Service, pp. 49-68. Institute for the study of Human Issues, Philadelphia.

Woodburn, James. 1981. Egalitarian Societies. In *Limited Wants, Unlimited Means, A Reader on Hunter-Gatherer Economics and the Environment*, edited by John Gowdy. pp 87-110, Island Press, Washington, DC.

Wylie, Alison. 1985. The reaction against analogy. *Advances in Method and Theory* 8: 63-111.

Wynn, Thomas, and Frederick L. Coolidge. 2012. *How to Think Like a Neandertal*. Oxford University Press, Oxford.

Wynn, Thomas, Frederick Coolidge and Martha Bright. 2009. Hohlenstein-Stadel and the Evolution of Human Conceptual Thought. *Cambridge Archaeological Journal*, 19(1), 73-84.

Yellen, John E. 1989. The Present and the Future of Hunter-Gatherer Studies. In *Archaeological Thought in America*, edited by C.C. Lamberg-Karlovsky, pp. 103-116. Cambridge University Press, Cambridge.

Yoffee, Norman and Andrew Sherratt. 1993. Introduction: The Sources of Archaeological Theory. In *Archaeological Theory: Who Sets the Agenda?* edited by N. Yoffee and A. Sherratt, pp. 1-10. Cambridge Unviersity Press, Cambridge.

Young, Biloine Whitting and Melvin L. Fowler. 2000. *Cahokia: The Great Native American Metropolis*. University of Illinois Press, Urbana and Chicago

Zappa, Frank. nd. BrainyQuote.com, Xplore Inc, 2018
https://www.brainyquote.com/quotes/frank_zappa_399512, accessed May6, 2018.

Zerzan, John. 1994. Future Primitive. In *Limited Wants, Unlimited Means, A Reader on Hunter-Gatherer Economics and the Environment*, edited by John Gowdy, pp. 255-280, Island Press, Washington, DC.

Ziman, John. 1988. What is Science? *In Introductory Readings in the Philosophy of Science*, edited by E. D. Klemke, et al., pp. 28-33. Prometheus Books, Buffalo.

LIST OF TABLES

Table 1	Origins	p. 28
Table 2	Southwest Asia and Mesopotamia	p. 70
Table 3	The Mediterranean	p. 80
Table 4	Europe	p. 86
Table 5	Egypt, Saharan and Sub-Saharan Africa	p. 94
Table 6	South and Southeast Asia	p. 104
Table 7	China and Central and East Asia	p. 112
Table 8	Australia and the Pacific	p. 120
Table 9	North America	p. 128
Table 10	Mesoamerica and the Caribbean	p. 136
Table 11	South America – Andes and Amazon	p. 148
Table 12	The Lakh Clock	p. 166

LIST OF FIGURES AND ILLUSTRATIONS

Cover Photo	Laetoli Footprints. Courtesy of Charles Musiba, 2018	Cover
Figure 1	Thinking Like an Anthropologist	p. 11
Figure 2	Tripliciter Sciendi Scenario	p. 21
Figure 3	Science Pyramid	p. 24
Figure 4	Science Pyramid and Culture	p. 25
Illustration 1	Acheulean Handaxe, Drawing by Greg Williams based on an sketch by John Frere c. 1800.	p. 34
Back Cover	Image by John Frere c. 1800. Frere, John: "Account of Flint Weapons Discovered at Hoxne in Suffolk", in Archeologia, vol. 13.- London, 1800.- Pp. 204-205, Public Domain, https://commons.wikimedia.org/w/index.php?curid=1602218 accessed 7-11-2018.	Back Cover

ABOUT THE AUTHOR

Gregory E. Williams earned his undergraduate degree in Anthropology/Archaeology from the University of Northern Colorado, and both a Master of Arts in Anthropology/Archaeology and a Master of Business Administration from the University of Colorado Denver. He is also a Registered Professional Archaeologist.

He has worked in public policy and on political campaigns on the federal, state and local levels in Washington, DC and various states over several decades. He currently owns and operates an association management company in Denver, Colorado and teaches archaeology part-time at various Colorado universities. His other research areas are rock-art and archaeoacoustics.

As someone with experience in business management, political campaigns, public policy, and archaeology, his perspective on prehistory is perhaps well-suited for the non-specialist in archaeology who is active in the ups and downs of the modern world but who also has an interest in our past.